HELD IN HIGH ESTEEM:

WOMEN COMMENDED BY PAUL

GENE & ELAINE GETZ

SERENDIPITY®
HOUSE

Held In High Esteem: Women Commended By Paul
© 2007 Gene and Elaine Getz

Published by Serendipity House Publishers
Nashville, Tennessee

ISBN: 1-5749-4335-1
Dewey Decimal Classification: 248.843
Subject Headings:
CHRISTIAN LIFE \ WOMEN \ WOMEN IN THE BIBLE

Scripture quotations marked HCSB taken from the *Holman Christian Standard Bible*®, Copyright © 1999, 2000, 2002, 2003 by Holman Bible Publishers. Used by permission.

Scriptures marked NASB from the *New American Standard Bible*®, © 1960, 1962, 1963, 1968, 1971, 1972, 1973, 1975, 1977, 1995 by the Lockman Foundation. Used by permission.

Scriptures marked NIV taken from the *Holy Bible, New International Version*, Copyright © 1973, 1978, 1984 by International Bible Society. Used by permission.

Scriptures marked MSG taken from the *THE MESSAGE*, Copyright © 1993, 1994, 1995, 1996, 2000, 2001, 2002. Used by permission of NavPress Publishing Group.

Scriptures marked NLT taken from the *The Holy Bible, New Living Translation*, Copyright © 1996. Used by permission of Tyndale House Publishers, Inc. Wheaton, IL 60189, USA. All rights reserved.

To purchase additional copies of this resource or other studies:
ORDER ONLINE at www.SerendipityHouse.com;
WRITE Serendipity House, 117 10th Avenue North, Nashville, TN 37234
FAX (615) 277-8181 ~ PHONE (800) 525-9563

1-800-525-9563
www.SerendipityHouse.com

Printed in the United States of America
13 12 11 10 09 08 07   1 2 3 4 5 6 7 8 9 10

Contents

Resource Credits   *4*

Held in High Esteem Introduction   *5*

Session	Title	Page
1	**EUNICE:** Leaving a Powerful Legacy of Faith	*6*
2	**LYDIA:** Stepping Out with a Willing Heart	*19*
3	**PHOEBE:** Serving Others for Christ	*32*
4	**PRISCILLA:** Living on the Edge	*46*
5	**JUNIA:** Developing Outstanding Character	*60*
6	**WOMEN OF HONOR:** Pointing Others to the Light	*73*

Leader's Guide

Required Session Supplies & Preparation	*90*
Leading a Small Group	*93*
Welcome to Community!	*96*
Group Covenant	*101*
About the Authors & Acknowledgments	*102*
Meeting Planner	*103*
Group Directory	*104*

Held in High Esteem

HOME...WORKS
MARRIAGE & FAMILY SERIES

Check these and other great studies
at www.SerendipityHouse.com ...

Some Assembly Required: Instructions for an Amazing Marriage

Dream Team: The Power of Two

Turning Up the Heat: Rekindle Romance and Passion

Coauthoring Your Child's Story: Parenting on Purpose

Can You Hear Me Now?: Communication in Marriage

Creating Mutual Funds: Financial Teamwork in Marriage

CREDITS

Serendipity House along with Gene and Elaine Getz wish to thank Regal Books, friends and partners in ministry, for graciously granting permission to include content from Gene and Elaine's book *The Measure of a Woman* in this Women of Purpose series.

HELD IN HIGH ESTEEM

WOMEN COMMENDED BY PAUL

Imagine what it must have been like to witness first-hand the ministry of Paul—his miraculous conversion and his passion that forever changed the world! The Bible gives us glimpses into the lives of amazing women who helped Paul take the gospel to the ends of the earth. These women were living letters of God's love, written to a lonely and loveless world. Each in her own unique way was a reflection of God's true nature and His true purpose for the people of the world.

The women Paul held in high regard longed to play a role in God's great redemptive story. As we walk alongside these ladies whom Paul so highly esteemed, let's determine to follow their examples by allowing our lives to point others to Jesus, too. There are people who will come to Christ, not because of philosophical debate or rational research, but because they see Jesus alive in us!

Held in High Esteem is a unique study for women, which blends fun elements, interactive discovery-focused Bible study, creative experiential activities, and wonderful opportunities to connect with God, with other women, and with your heart. Journal pages are provided with each session to support you in taking some of your deepest longings and questions to your heart and to God. Gather some gems from the lives of each of these devoted women:

* Eunice and Lois – leaving a powerful legacy of faith
* Lydia – stepping out with a willing heart
* Phoebe – serving others for Christ
* Priscilla – living on the edge
* Junia – developing outstanding character
* Women of Honor – pointing others to the light

The Women of Purpose series highlights ordinary women used by God in extraordinary ways. As we delve below the surface and into the hearts of these women, we discover not only who they are, but also who *we* are. We find our hearts awakening to deeper intimacy with God and to an increasing desire to give ourselves to something grand, noble, and bigger than ourselves. We don't have to settle for simply existing; God created us to really live—to be women of passion and women of purpose.

EUNICE: LEAVING A POWERFUL LEGACY OF FAITH

Most of us have pearls in our jewelry boxes. Over the years, people have come up with all kinds of tests to distinguish fake pearls from real ones. Some say you can tell by rubbing the pearls against your teeth; fake pearls feel smooth, and real pearls feel gritty. Some argue a pearl's authenticity is best discovered under bright light. Fake pearls don't reflect light well. They lack the brilliant shine and varied colors of real pearls. Only authentic pearls, full of imperfections and irregularities, beautifully reflect light.[1]

The authenticity of our faith can be measured similarly—by how well we reflect the light of Jesus. Many things get passed down through families—jewelry, inside jokes, nicknames, chicken pox. But the most important thing passed on to our biological and spiritual children is a spiritual legacy of authentic faith. Those who come behind us will shine brightly if we help them experience the life of Jesus and reflect His light. Eunice teaches us the vital importance of our legacy to the next generation.

BREAKING THE ICE - *10-15 Minutes*

LEADER: These "Breaking the Ice" activities and questions are designed to get people talking. Encourage each group member to participate but be sure to keep things moving. This activity helps group members get acquainted with one another.

INSTRUCTIONS FOR THE GROUP EXPERIENCE: Before the group meeting, trace a life-size figure of a woman on each of two large pieces of butcher paper. Label one "Hypocrite Hannah" and the other "Sincere Sharise." Tape the cutouts up at the front of the room. Bring colored markers.

1. Take turns around the group introducing yourselves and briefly describing your families.

2. What family story, habit, or heirloom has been passed down over many generations in your family?

3. As a group, brainstorm 10 things parents can do to contribute to a child's becoming hypocritical or spiritually apathetic. Write these on the Hypocrite Hannah cutout using the markers provided.

4. Now, as a group, brainstorm ten ways parents can raise children to be sincere in their faith. Write these suggestions on the Sincere Sharise cutout.

DISCOVERING THE TRUTH
25-30 Minutes

LEADER: For "Discovering the Truth," ask various group members to read the Bible passages aloud. Be sure to leave time for the "Embracing the Truth" and "Connecting" segments that follow this discussion.

RECOGNIZING A VITAL ROLE

The Apostle Paul wrote to his spiritual son Timothy not long before Paul's death at the hands of Emperor Nero's Roman guards. As the aging preacher sat in a cold, dark prison cell and contemplated his impending martyrdom, he remembered with joy his precious friend and the ministry they had shared. Paul knew Timothy might follow in his footsteps, spending the rest of his life facing rejection, beatings, imprisonment, or even death. And so Paul wrote a letter to encourage young Timothy by reminding him of the faith and example of his precious mother, Eunice, and grandmother, Lois. Paul highlighted the priority of passing on a legacy of sincere faith and spiritual vitality to the next generation.

¹ Paul, an apostle of Christ Jesus by God's will, for the promise of life in Christ Jesus:
² To Timothy, my dearly loved child. Grace, mercy, and peace from God the Father and Christ Jesus our Lord.
³ I thank God, whom I serve with a clear conscience as my forefathers did, when I constantly remember you in my prayers night and day.
⁴ Remembering your tears, I long to see you so that I may be filled with joy,
⁵ clearly recalling your sincere faith that first lived in your grandmother Lois, then in your mother Eunice, and that I am convinced is in you also.
⁶ Therefore, I remind you to keep ablaze the gift of God that is in you through the laying on of my hands.
⁷ For God has not given us a spirit of fearfulness, but one of power, love, and sound judgment.

2 TIMOTHY 1:1-7, HCSB

LEADER: *Discuss as many discovery questions as time permits. Encourage participation by inviting different individuals to respond. It will help to highlight in advance the questions you don't want to miss. Be familiar with the Scripture Notes at the end of this session.*

1. According to Paul, what were some characteristics that he cherished in Timothy? How do you think Lois and Eunice so powerfully influenced Timothy's spiritual growth?

2. In your view, what attitudes characterize spiritual authenticity? Why are these attitudes essential to authentic spirituality?

The word used for "sincere" in this passage is *anypokritos*. Its opposite is the root of our word "hypocrite." When Paul writes that "sincere faith" lived first in Timothy's mother Eunice, and also in his grandmother Lois, he uses a Greek verb that literally means, "to make its home inside." Sincere faith in God, an invaluable legacy passed from one generation to the next, literally made its home in the hearts of Lois and Eunice.

3. Describe a person you know like Eunice or Lois who allows faith to make its home in his or her heart.

Timothy's name means "one who fears God," so we can be confident that his mother and grandmother planned to raise him in the faith even before his birth.[2] Clearly the women were intentional about the spiritual legacy they planned to sow in his life. Even his name was meant to remind him of the importance of placing God first in his life.

4. What challenges can we face in leading younger believers to grow in authentic faith? How can we avoid hypocritical or surface faith?

Principle for Living

The most important thing you as a parent can do is to raise your children to know and love the Lord. Even those who don't have children, however, are responsible for helping to train up young believers, continuously determining to pass on sincere faith and godly wisdom to each generation.

BEING THE MODEL

[14] *But as for you, continue in what you have learned and firmly believed, knowing those from whom you learned,* [15] *and that from childhood you have known the sacred Scriptures, which are able to instruct you for salvation through faith in Christ Jesus.*

2 TIMOTHY 3:14-15, HCSB

5. Modeling and instruction from Eunice and Lois shaped Timothy for a strong life of faith and ministry. What methods can we can use to introduce young children to Jesus and the Scriptures? Why is it important that we make the effort?

It's easy to assume that since Timothy's mother and grandmother were both stout followers of Jesus, he had little choice but to personally adopt the faith. The Book of Acts, however, paints a picture of Timothy's family background that opposes that theory:

¹ (Paul) came to Derbe and then to Lystra, where a disciple named Timothy lived, whose mother was a Jewess and a believer, but whose father was a Greek. ² The brothers at Lystra and Iconium spoke well of him. ³ Paul wanted to take (Timothy) along on the journey, so he circumcised him because of the Jews who lived in that area, for they all knew that his father was a Greek.

ACTS 16:1-3, NIV

Timothy's mother was a believer, but we can infer from Acts 16 that his father was not a Christ-follower. Because there's no other reference to the influence of Timothy's father on his life, we can assume that Eunice and Lois had to serve as the primary spiritual influences for the boy. His father may even have discouraged Timothy from following Christ. After all, Christianity was viewed with suspicion and persecution in Timothy's world.

6. What effects can a spouse's opposition or apathy to spiritual things have on a child? On a marriage?

7. What challenges are unique to moms who are the primary spiritual influence in their children's lives? How can the people in your church support those women who are alone in providing spiritual foundations for their children?

Eunice raised her precious son to have a sincere faith in the Lord. Even at a young age, he showed great spiritual maturity because his mother had planted a vital faith in God in his young heart. When Timothy became a missionary partner with Paul in spreading the gospel across the world, it's likely his mother felt inner assurance that she had done well.

EMBRACING THE TRUTH
15-20 Minutes

LEADER: *This section focuses on helping group members integrate what they've learned from the Bible into their own hearts and lives. Invite volunteers to read the Bible passages.*

LIVING YOUR LEGACY

Perhaps now more than ever, cultural trends can devastate families. That's why Christian mothers—as Eunice did—must determine to provide their children with a vital, sincere faith in God and in God's role for their lives. Grasping perspective on living your legacy is a great place to start.

³ Similarly, teach the older women to live in a way that honors God. They must not slander others or be heavy drinkers. Instead, they should teach others what is good.
⁴ These older women must train the younger women to love their husbands and their children, ⁵ to live wisely and be pure, to work in their homes, to do good, and to be submissive to their husbands. Then they will not bring shame on the word of God.

TITUS 2:3-5, NLT

1. What part of Titus 2:3-5 most speaks to you as you consider your role within your home? What, if anything, do you need to change about your attitude toward your home and family?

2. How can a mother in our culture manage all the pressures and responsibilities of child-rearing?

Session One

⁷ Train yourself in godliness, ⁸ for, the training of the body has a limited benefit, but godliness is beneficial in every way, since it holds promise for the present life and also for the life to come. ⁹ This saying is trustworthy and deserves full acceptance. ¹⁰ In fact, we labor and strive for this, because we have put our hope in the living God, who is the Savior of everyone, especially of those who believe. ¹¹ Command and teach these things. ¹² No one should despise your youth; instead, you should be an example to the believers in speech, in conduct, in love, in faith, in purity. ¹³ Until I come, give your attention to public reading, exhortation, and teaching. ¹⁴ Do not neglect the gift that is in you; it was given to you through prophecy, with the laying on of hands by the council of elders. ¹⁵ Practice these things; be committed to them, so that your progress may be evident to all. ¹⁶ Be conscientious about yourself and your teaching; persevere in these things, for by doing this you will save both yourself and your hearers.

1 TIMOTHY 4:7B-16, HCSB

3. Review 1 Timothy 4:7-16 and discuss attitudes and actions that Paul encourages for training in godliness.

4. In what ways do you "train yourself for godliness"? How are you using the spiritual gifts God has given you? Do your children see your godly training and your use of your spiritual gifts? If so, explain.

Principle for Living

A parent's example is like a branding iron that will leave its imprint on a child's beliefs, habits, and character. Therefore, you must be intentional in helping children and others in your care to experience the wonder of God and to learn His ways.

A ENDURING LEGACY

Not long after the massive exodus from Egypt, Moses shared God's instructions for creating an enduring legacy with the fledgling Israelite community. We can learn so much today from these instructions ...

⁹ Only be on your guard and diligently watch yourselves, so that you don't forget the things your eyes have seen and so that they don't slip from your mind as long as you live. Teach them to your children and your grandchildren. ¹⁰ The day you stood before the LORD your God at Horeb, the LORD said to me, 'Assemble the people before Me, and I will let them hear My words, so that they may learn to fear Me all the days they live on the earth and may instruct their children.

DEUTERONOMY 4:9-10, HCSB

5. What's the significance of passing the experience of God on to grand-children as well as to children? What does this tell us about God's plan for the redemption of creation?

6. Why do you think God warns us about slipping and forgetfulness? What do you think it means to "fear the Lord"? How does a proper fear of the Lord motivate us to instruct those who come behind us?

Proverbs 9:10 says, *"Fear of the Lord is the beginning of wisdom."* "Fear" in this case means to marvel at or be in awe of God's incredible power and beauty—His total "otherness." Theologians call this "transcendence." God is so extraordinary that no one or nothing else even comes close. He's beyond powerful and glorious. He's eternal, immortal, full of wonder, and totally desirable.

Principle for Living
*Just as new life emerged from Eunice's and Lois' deep journey of faith
and flowed out to Timothy and all those he touched,
you must take the journey of faith and light the way for those who follow.
It all begins with fear and awe of the One who is above all and in all and through all.*

CONNECTING
10-15 Minutes

LEADER: Use "Connecting" as a time to begin to bond with, encourage, and support one another. Invite everyone to join in the discussions. Set the tone of openness by sharing your struggles first.

1. In what ways do you struggle with putting on a mask or being insincere in your faith? How do you think hiding behind your mask or false self affects your relationship with God?

2. Why does it seem easy to get away with an insincere faith at church? How can wearing our masks and playing at spirituality impact our churches and those who will come behind us?

3. In what ways can we challenge each other to increase in emotional and spiritual authenticity? Share ideas for moving down the path toward sincere, from-the-heart faith in God.

LEADER: Take some time to look together at the Group Covenant at the back of the book (page 101). Now is the time for each person to pass around her book to collect contact information on the Group Directory on page 104.

Share prayer requests that you will pray over between now and the next session. In addition, pray that God will strengthen and encourage each woman as she takes her heart's questions to God this week. *How can the members of this group pray for you as you strive to leave a legacy of faith?*

TAKING IT HOME

LEADER: Explain that the "Taking It Home" section contains introspective questions as well as questions to take to God. Encourage each person to set aside quiet time this week, so she can make the most of this study and group experience. Be sure to highlight the importance of writing down thoughts, feelings, and key insights that God reveals. Journaling is a powerful tool.

Studying God's truth is not an end in itself. Our goal is always heart and life change. To take the next step of integrating truth into our lives, we need to (1) look honestly into our hearts to understand the true motivations that drive us and (2) seek God's perspective on our lives. Psalm 51:6, NASB, says God "desire[s] truth in the innermost being."

A QUESTION TO TAKE TO MY HEART

The following question asks you to look into your heart and focus on your deepest feelings about yourself. Our behaviors are the best indicators of what we really believe deep down. Look deep into the underlying beliefs in your heart where your truest attitudes and motivations live. Spend some time reflecting and don't settle for a quick answer.

❧ *Which is more "at home" in my heart: Jesus and His values or the values of the culture with its self-focus? What do my attitudes and actions show me that I hold most dear?*

A QUESTION TO TAKE TO GOD

When you ask God a question, expect His Spirit to guide your heart to discover His truth. Be careful not to rush or manufacture an answer. Don't write down what you think the "right answer" is. Don't turn the Bible into a spiritual reference book or encyclopedia. Just pose a question to God and wait on Him. Remember, the litmus test for anything we hear from God is alignment with the Bible as our ultimate truth source. Keep a journal of the insights you gain from your time with God.

❧ *God, you know me better than I know myself. What's the legacy You want me to leave imprinted in the lives of others?*

Scripture Notes

2 TIMOTHY 1:1-7; 3:14-15

1:1-2 Paul ... to Timothy. Paul's greeting in his letter to Titus (which was probably written between 1 and 2 Timothy) was longer than usual (Titus 1:1-4). Here he returns to a briefer, more typical opening.

1:4 Remembering your tears. Paul is probably recalling that when they parted the last time, he was to go on to Macedonia while Timothy stayed in Ephesus (see Acts 20:37 for a similar situation). *I long to see you.* This is the main reason he writes this letter: to urge Timothy to join him (4:9). *joy.* Once again, as he did in the Philippian letter, Paul sounds a note of joy even though he is in prison.

1:5 Eunice. Timothy's mother was a Jewish Christian (Acts 16:1). His father was a Gentile, probably not a believer.

1:6 keep ablaze. "Rekindle." Paul uses the image of a fire, not to suggest that his spiritual gift has "gone out," but that it needs constant stirring up so that it always burns brightly. *the gift of God.* Paul reminds Timothy not only of his spiritual roots (the faith of his mother and grandmother), but also of the gift he has been given for ministry.

1:7 spirit of fearfulness. Paul makes this sort of appeal because Timothy is not a forceful person (1 Tim. 4:12). *Power, love, and sound judgment.* The gift the Spirit gave Timothy leads not to fearfulness, but to these positive characteristics. All Christians have been given this same spirit of power, love, and sound judgment.

3:15 instruct you for salvation through faith in Christ Jesus. The Old Testament Scriptures lead one to salvation; i.e., to an understanding and experience of God's saving purpose.

ACTS 16:1-3

16:1-3 circumcised him. As the son of a Jewish woman, Jewish law said that Timothy ought to have been circumcised as an infant. Perhaps his Gentile father (who apparently was dead at the time of Paul's visit) had forbidden it. Perhaps, since there is no mention of a synagogue in Lystra, his mother had not been able to practice the Jewish traditions very seriously (her marriage to a Gentile was also a violation of Jewish law). At any rate, for Paul to allow Timothy, a Jew, to accompany him apart from following the age-old Jewish custom of circumcision would communicate to other Jews that he had no regard whatsoever for their honored traditions. To avoid that offense, Timothy was circumcised. This is a further illustration of Paul's (and Timothy's) willingness to accommodate himself to cultural sensitivities.

Session One

TITUS 2:3-5

2:3 teach others what is good. Formal instruction is probably not intended. Rather, the idea is that the older women would mentor, modeling "what is good" for younger women in terms of a woman's character and in her role as a wife and mother.

2:5 submissive to their husbands. Paul is not placing women under the authority of all men. Instead he has in mind submission to the woman's own husband.

1 TIMOTHY 4:7-16

4:7 silly myths. Having told Timothy to hold on to what is true, Paul now warns him to avoid what is false. *train yourself in godliness.* In contrast to the unchristian asceticism (v. 3), Paul now proposes a genuinely Christian form of self-discipline.

4:8 training of the body. While affirming the value of physical exercise, Paul's real interest is in spiritual exercise ("godliness"). *promise for the present life and also for the life to come.* The "life" Paul refers to is the "eternal life" one receives through belief in Jesus (1:16). It is this quality of life—in the present and the future—that is promised to those who believe in and know Jesus (John 17:3).

4:11 Command. Paul instructs that Timothy must speak with authority. The impression given here in verses 11-12 and elsewhere (1 Cor. 16:10-11; 2 Tim. 1:6-9) is that Timothy was a somewhat diffident, even timid, person.

4:12 youth. The problem may have to do with Timothy's age. He is probably only in his early 30s. Yet, he is living in a culture that respects age. *be an example.* There is little he can do about his age, but Timothy can lead by example. Paul identifies five areas in which he is to model Christian conduct. "Speech" and "conduct" refer to day-by-day conversation and behavior. "Love" (agape), "faith" (faithfulness), and "purity" (not only chastity but general integrity) refer to inner qualities that show themselves by an outer lifestyle.

4:13 public reading. This is the first reference to the use of Scripture in Christian worship, although this was common in Jewish worship. *teaching.* This is instruction in Christian doctrine.

4:14 laying on of hands. Appointment to office (ordination) was accompanied by the laying on of hands (literally, the "pressing of hands") by the commissioning body (here, the elders).

SESSION QUOTATIONS

1 www.beautyanswer.com/Fashion-Accessories/2690-fashion.html accessed 6/15/07.

2 Herbert Lockyer, *All the Women of the Bible*, (Grand Rapids, MI: Zondervan, 1967), p. 54.

Session One

LYDIA: STEPPING OUT WITH A WILLING HEART

In Acts 16:6-15 Paul and his missionary companions had trouble deciding where to go next in sharing the good news about Jesus and His resurrection. The Spirit of God prevented them from sharing in the towns of Bithynia and Troas, instead encouraging them, via a vision, to head to Philippi. Though the missionaries obeyed the vision, they were probably surprised to find not a group of learned men eager to hear their message, but a group of women. As Paul and the others shared about the hope and redemption in Jesus, a woman named Lydia instantly believed in Jesus. Lydia went home, shared the story of Jesus with her household, and the entire family was baptized. Lydia's attitude of openness to God gives a great example of how we should live: with our hearts standing in readiness to embrace God and His plan.

BREAKING THE ICE - *10-15 Minutes*

LEADER: These "Breaking the Ice" questions are designed to get people to become better acquainted and to hear their own voices. Encourage each group member to participate, but be sure to keep things moving.

1. What part of your life are you most likely to neglect in times of extreme busyness? Why? What would happen if you made this often-neglected part of your life a priority?

2. In what setting, outside church, are you best able to connect with and worship God? What is it about that setting that helps you to be more in tune with God's Spirit?

3. What did you discover in your "Taking It Home" time this past week? What did you hear from God about your values and your legacy?

DISCOVERING THE TRUTH

20-25 Minutes

A HUNGER FOR GOD

In Matthew 5:6 Jesus said, "Blessed are those who hunger and thirst for righteousness, because they will be filled" (HCSB). Let's look at the following passage to see how Jesus' words apply to Lydia.

[13] On the Sabbath day we went outside the city gate by the river, where we thought there was a place of prayer. We sat down and spoke to the women gathered there.
[14] A woman named Lydia, a dealer in purple cloth from the city of Thyatira, who worshiped God, was listening. The Lord opened her heart to pay attention to what was spoken by Paul.
[15] After she and her household were baptized, she urged us, "If you consider me a believer in the Lord, come and stay at my house." And she persuaded us.

ACTS 16:13-15, HCSB

Session Two

1. What can we determine about Lydia's personal and professional life from Acts 16:14-15?

2. What do you find significant about the fact that Lydia was with others at a "place of prayer" and that she "worshiped God" before her encounter with the missionaries?

3. According to verse 14, how can we explain Lydia's openness to hear and act so quickly on the words of Paul? What does this tell you about how God was working in Lydia's life?

4. What did Lydia do to show her gratitude to Paul and the other missionaries? What does this act of hospitality suggest about her willingness to adventure into the unfamiliar with God?

Lydia's story illustrates that God is always drawing us to Himself. He made us in His image and created us for a deep relationship with Him. He set up a special role for each one of us to play in the redemption of the world. Lydia's story demonstrates that when we live with hearts open to God's will, He will give us new life and will reveal the purpose of our lives.

Principle for Living
You are incredibly special to God. When you open yourself up to His influence on your life, you will encounter God in ways that will rock your world.

WILLING TO MAKE A STAND

Lydia was a successful businesswoman in a time and place where business was largely dominated by men. She owned an enterprise that sold purple cloth—its purple dye being the most rare and expensive dye of that time reserved for those of wealth, nobility, or royalty.

5. Paul and Silas were often beaten and thrown into prison throughout the empire for the message they taught. How could Lydia's becoming a Christ-follower have negatively affected her business and family?

³⁵ *When daylight came, the chief magistrates sent the police to say, "Release those men!"*
³⁶ *The jailer reported these words to Paul: "The magistrates have sent orders for you to be released. So come out now and go in peace."*
³⁷ *But Paul said to them, "They beat us in public without a trial, although we are Roman citizens, and threw us in jail. And now are they going to smuggle us out secretly? Certainly not! On the contrary, let them come themselves and escort us out!"*
³⁸ *Then the police reported these words to the magistrates. And they were afraid when they heard that Paul and Silas were Roman citizens.*
³⁹ *So they came and apologized to them, and escorting them out, they urged them to leave town.*
⁴⁰ *After leaving the jail, they came to Lydia's house where they saw and encouraged the brothers, and departed.*

ACTS 16:35-40, HCSB

6. Why do you think Paul and Silas went to Lydia's house after their release? Who did they expect to find gathered at her home? What do these verses tell you about Lydia's ministry after her baptism?

Imagine you are a high-profile businesswoman in your city. Paul and Silas, bruised, in trouble with the authorities, and recently-released from jail, show up at your house and ask to spend the night.

7. What concerns might you have about opening your home to them, including the effect on your standing in the community? What would you have to believe about God and His will for your life in order to welcome them graciously?

Lydia never shied away from the danger associated with becoming a Christ-follower. Instead, she opened her home as the gathering place for the fledgling church in Thyatira and Philippi. She even welcomed her brothers in the Lord by opening her home as a refuge. Doing so clearly proclaimed her allegiance to God and her determination to love others as Jesus would.

Principle for Living

Lydia willingly used her resources to show others God's love and provision. How you use your home, money, and resources to benefit others is an indicator of how seriously you take your relationship with God and how courageous you are in pursuing the adventure He's laid out for you.

EMBRACING THE TRUTH
20-25 Minutes

LEADER: *This section focuses on helping group members integrate what they've learned from the Bible into their own hearts and lives. Invite volunteers to read the Bible passages.*

CROSSING OVER TO NEW LIFE

As a responsible businesswoman, Lydia was used to making major decisions quickly. She thought in terms of cost-benefit analysis. Therefore, it's not surprising that when she was presented with the message of salvation and new life through believing in Jesus Christ as Lord and Savior, she made an instant, life-changing, and far-reaching decision: to accept Jesus' gift of new life and to devote her life to serving Him.

Lydia had to make choices and adjustments as she entered her new life in Christ, just as the Israelites did as they entered new life in the Promised Land. Joshua, the leader of the Israelites, also shows us a wonderful model of a courage and willingness to follow God no matter what the costs. Before he died, Joshua challenged the people to live for God in the Promised Land:

14 Therefore, fear the LORD and worship Him in sincerity and truth. Get rid of the gods your ancestors worshiped beyond the Euphrates River and in Egypt, and worship the LORD. 15 But if it doesn't please you to worship the LORD, choose for yourselves today the one you will worship: the gods your fathers worshiped beyond the Euphrates River, or the gods of the Amorites in whose land you are living. As for me and my family, we will worship the LORD.

JOSHUA 24:14-15, HCSB

1. Even though God had given them a life that they did not deserve, many Israelites in the end did not follow God. Why do you think we tend to give our lives and loyalties to lesser "gods" like comfort, convenience, and security?

2. How did you come to know Jesus as your Savior and Lord? What key experiences or conversations led up to your choice to submit your life to Him? What was the deal clincher for you?

3. What do you think it means to worship God in "sincerity and truth" (verse 14)? In what ways can we extend our worship into our everyday lives in the same way as Lydia and others in the early church?

Session Two

4. Just like Joshua (verse 15), when you make a choice for one course of action, you're also choosing to go against other courses. What does your choice to follow Jesus exclude from your life? How do you deal with giving up these other options?

Principle for Living

In order to experience all that God has for you, you must make a personal choice to join Jesus in His mission and embrace your new life in Him. This will require stepping out of your comfort zone and your complacency.

ALLOWING FAITH TO PERMEATE LIFE

The Bible is full of practical advice on how to live out our relationship with Jesus so that our faith permeates every area of our lives. Here are a couple examples ...

[9] Love must be without hypocrisy. Detest evil; cling to what is good. [10] Show family affection to one another with brotherly love. Outdo one another in showing honor. [11] Do not lack diligence; be fervent in spirit; serve the Lord. [12] Rejoice in hope; be patient in affliction; be persistent in prayer. [13] Share with the saints in their needs; pursue hospitality.

ROMANS 12:9-13, HCSB

[7] Now the end of all things is near; therefore, be clear-headed and disciplined for prayer. [8] Above all, keep your love for one another at full strength, since love covers a multitude of sins. [9] Be hospitable to one another without complaining.

1 PETER 4:7-9, HCSB

5. How can we in the church love each other *with* "hypocrisy" (counter to Romans 12:9)? List some key attitudes and actions from Romans 12:9-13 and 1 Peter 4:7-11 that lead us to sincere love.

6. What causes us to withhold hospitality? What causes us to complain about providing hospitality to others as 1 Peter 4:9 instructs?

7. What do you need from God and from fellow believers in order to keep your love for others "at full strength" (1 Peter 4:8)?

Love; clinging to good; family affection; honor; diligence; fervent in spirit; rejoicing; hope; patience; prayer; hospitality; clear-headed discipline ... all life-giving words and all words we should experience in the everyday life of an authentic, Christian community!

CONNECTING *-10-15 Minutes*

LEADER: Use "Connecting" as a time to begin to develop closeness, encourage, and support one another. Invite everyone to join in the discussions and to be comfortable with who God created them to be.

MANAGING GOD'S LIFE GIFTS

Lydia's faith was deeply personal but, at the same time, profoundly interpersonal. Her personal faith in Jesus was lived out in the context of community. She used the resources God had given her to build up others in the faith and to reach out to those outside the faith.

1. As you consider the way you live out faith in community, look again at the list of attitudes and actions that lead us to sincere love (Romans 12:9-13 and 1 Peter 4:7-11). In which of these areas do you need to develop so you can experience sincere love inside or outside the church? Explain.

[10] *Based on the gift they have received, everyone should use it to serve others, as good managers of the varied grace of God.* [11] *If anyone speaks, his speech should be like the oracles of God; if anyone serves, his service should be from the strength God provides, so that in everything God may be glorified through Jesus Christ. To Him belong the glory and the power forever and ever. Amen.*

1 PETER 4:10-11, HCSB

2. What are some spiritual gifts, varied resources, and experiences God has given you that you can use to serve others and give glory to God?

Principle for Living
God gave you special and unique gifts so that you would use them to involve yourself in His mission to rescue people who need hope and healing and to build up others in the faith. It's poor management to squander those gifts.

LEADER INSTRUCTIONS FOR THE GROUP EXPERIENCE: Provide one 6" x 6" square of red cloth and a fabric pen for each participant. Pass around a piece of crimson cloth and a fabric pen to each woman. Ask group members to draw a heart on one side of the cloth. Then have them list inside the heart all the blessings they have received from giving their lives to Jesus. The backside of the cloth should be used as a place to write the names of those with whom they desire to share the life and hope found in Jesus Christ. Separate the women into small groups and ask them to share what they wrote on their pieces of cloth before praying together for one another.

Pray together for the names on the crimson cloths. Pray also that God will strengthen and encourage each woman as she takes her heart's questions to God this week. *How can this group pray for your courage and conviction?*

PRAYER REQUESTS:

Session Two

TAKING IT HOME

A QUESTION TO TAKE TO MY HEART

The following question asks you to look into your heart and focus on your deepest feelings about yourself. Our behaviors are the best indicators of what we really believe deep down. Look deep into the underlying beliefs down in your heart where your truest attitudes and motivations live. Spend some time reflecting and don't settle for a quick answer.

    ❖ *What do my priorities reveal about my willingness to join God on the journey He has marked out for me? What fears or attitudes keep me from stepping out the way Lydia did?*

Session Two

A Question to Take to God

When you ask God a question, expect His Spirit to guide your heart to discover His truth. Be careful not to rush or manufacture an answer. Don't write down what you think the "right answer" is. Don't turn the Bible into a spiritual reference book or encyclopedia. Just pose a question to God and wait on Him. Remember, the litmus test for anything we hear from God is alignment with the Bible as our ultimate truth source. Keep a journal of the insights you gain from your time with God.

Lord, how have You been trying to connect with me recently? How have I been closing myself off to You and Your purposes in my life?

SCRIPTURE NOTES

ACTS 16:13-15, 35-40

16:13 a place of prayer. Ten men were required in order to form a synagogue. The fact that there was no synagogue in Philippi indicates how small the Jewish population was. *outside the city gate by the river.* The Jews may have been forbidden to meet inside the city limits, or they may have wanted to be near a river to perform their ceremonial washings.

16:14-15 Lydia. Macedonian women enjoyed far more freedom and opportunities than many of their counterparts elsewhere. Lydia was a businesswoman involved in selling purple cloth, a luxury item indicating that she was a woman of wealth. *Thyatira.* A city in the province of Asia noted for its cloth dyeing industry. Evidence indicates that there was a Jewish community in Thyatira, which probably influenced Lydia towards faith in the God of the Jews.

16:35-40 The magistrates simply wanted to expel Paul and Silas from town to avoid any further trouble. However, they refused to go without a personal apology from the magistrates for their breach of justice. This was not simply a matter of self-vindication, nor a matter of insisting on the proper administration of justice. It was especially important for the protection of the young church in Philippi since Paul's claim to citizenship showed he was not interested in violating Roman customs as he had been charged (v. 21).

By being escorted out of the prison by the magistrates, a signal would be communicated to the community at large that the charges had been false. As a result, the community would be more likely to leave the young church alone.

JOSHUA 24:14-15

24:1-33 The credits rolling at the end of Joshua's life repeat a common theme: God alone had achieved the victory for Israel. From Abraham to the present moment, Joshua's review of history centered on God's faithfulness to His people. In the context of the past, Joshua provided Israel with an ultimatum for the future. Israel must respond wholeheartedly and serve the Lord alone.

24:14 fear the LORD. No single English word conveys every aspect of the word "fear" in this phrase. The meaning includes worshipful submission, reverential awe, and obedient respect to the covenant-keeping God of Israel. *Get rid of the gods.* Even after all that the Lord had done during the exodus, wilderness wandering, and conquest of Canaan, some Israelites clung to the gods their ancestors had worshiped either in Mesopotamia or Egypt.

24:15 As for me … we will worship. One man registered his vote for the supremacy of God. Although he was their leader, Joshua knew that he could not speak for Israel. The choice to serve God must be a personal decision.

ROMANS 12:9-13

12:9 Love. The Greek word agape: self-giving love in action on behalf of others, which is made possible by God's Spirit. *without hypocrisy.* Genuine, not counterfeit or showy.

12:10 brotherly love. The word for love used here, *philadelphia*, denotes the tender affection found in families, now said to be appropriate to those in the church—which is the Christian's (follower of Christ's) new family. *honor.* Since other Christians are in union with Christ, they are to be honored.

12:11 be fervent. The Greek word for "fervent" is also used of water when it has been brought to a boil (or of metal, like copper, which is glowing red-hot in refining or shaping).

1 PETER 4:7-11

4:10 gift. This word is *charisma* and refers to the different gifts that the Holy Spirit gives to individual Christians for the sake of the whole body. *to serve others.* The point of these gifts is to use them for the sake of others. *varied grace of God.* Each one has a gift, but not all have the same gift (see also Rom 12:6-8; 1 Cor. 12:7-10; and Eph. 4:11-12 for lists of various gifts).

4:11 Peter discusses two gifts in particular: the gift of teaching and preaching, and the gift of service. *If anyone speaks.* This is not the gift of tongues (the speaking of other languages or ecstatic utterance), nor the gift of prophecy, but ordinary teaching and preaching. *If anyone serves.* There are different kinds of service: helping those in need, giving leadership, providing money, etc. (Acts 6:1-4; Rom 12:13; 1 Cor. 12:5).

Session Two

PHOEBE: SERVING OTHERS FOR CHRIST

Imagine the following advertisement on your church's marquee:

"Wanna be a servant? We can show you how!"

How do you think your congregation would respond to such a claim? What would you think of such words? Do you think the sign would lead people in your community to knock down the church doors in a rush to get in or would it more likely keep them out? Modern cultural values and attitudes often clash with the idea of servanthood. Few popular magazines, radio shows, and television programs bother to extol the joys of being a helper, much less a servant. Instead, our culture gives constant advice on what it takes to be successful, seemingly fulfilled, and independent.

Today's paths to success often leave us flat and unfulfilled. A look at the life of Phoebe, an early Christ-follower, may convince us that joyful service to others—not so much time thinking of ourselves—is what life is all about.

BREAKING THE ICE - *10-15 Minutes*

LEADER: These "Breaking the Ice" experiences will help group members continue to develop closeness within you group and also ease into the topic of servanthood and success. Keep this time lighthearted and fun.

HITTING THE BIG TIME

1. Pretend you are an evil Dr. Frankenstein. Your job is to create an ineffective, harmful leader who will take over the world. What five characteristics of a really bad leader would you use as a basis for your design?

2. Pair off with another group member. Look together through a couple of the magazines provided. Cut out titles and sentences that seem to embody our culture's philosophy of a "Successful Woman." Paste these to a piece of construction paper and then present them to the group.

3. In your "Taking It Home" assignment, were you surprised that your willingness to follow God slips at times? What insights did you gain about areas where you close God off or about fears that keep you from following hard after God?

DISCOVERING THE TRUTH
20-25 Minutes

PHOEBE'S LIFE OF RADIANCE

Though the Bible says little about Phoebe, the information it does give offers an insightful and inspiring look into the life of one of Paul's effective and influential coworkers in the developing early church.

¹ I commend to you our sister Phoebe, who is a servant of the church in Cenchrea.
² I ask you to receive her in the Lord in a way worthy of the saints and to give her any help she may need from you, for she has been a great help to many people, including me.

ROMANS 16:1-2, NIV

LEADER: Discuss as many discovery questions as time permits. Encourage participation by inviting different individuals to respond. It will help to highlight in advance the questions you don't want to miss. Be familiar with the Scripture Notes at the end of this session.

1. Reflect on Paul's words about Phoebe in Romans 16:1-2. What clues do you see about why he was able to commend her so highly?

2. Why do you think Paul used Phoebe's service record as an introduction to his request that the church in Rome help her?

Phoebe was probably a woman of wealth and influence who had given her life for God's kingdom. Phoebe's name means "radiant" and is derived from the feminine form of a name given to the Greek god Apollo. Likely Phoebe had been converted from a pagan background, but after her new birth in Christ, Phoebe's life reflected the radiant joy and love of Jesus. It's likely that it was Phoebe who carried Paul's letter to the Romans, perhaps because of her radiance and because of Paul's confidence in her dedication.

⁴ I sought the LORD, and He answered me and delivered me from all my fears. ⁵ Those who look to Him are radiant with joy; their faces will never be ashamed.

PSALM 34:4-5, HCSB

3. We often seem to do the reverse of Psalm 34:4—we hide from the Lord. What wrong views of God prevent us from seeking Him? How can our relationship with God keep us radiant even in uncertain or difficult times?

Session Three

Phoebe's home of Cenchrea was a Roman city not far from Corinth that was also permeated with pagan practices. In his letter to the Ephesians, Paul describes the pagan mind-set found in places like Cenchrea:

18 They are darkened in their understanding, excluded from the life of God, because of the ignorance that is in them and because of the hardness of their hearts. 19 They became callous and gave themselves over to promiscuity for the practice of every kind of impurity with a desire for more and more.

EPHESIANS 4:18-19, HCSB

4. Given a culture like the one described in Ephesians 4, how do you think Phoebe's approach to helping others could have proved beneficial inside and outside of the church?

The word translated "help" or "benefactor" in Romans 16:2 is the Greek word *prostatis*, "a word used in classical Greek of trainers who dedicated themselves to assist an athlete competing for a prize."[1]

5. How important is the role of a trainer to the success of an athlete? How might Paul's commendation of Phoebe have changed had she lived out the kind of "successful, independent" attitude so prevalent in our culture?

Principle for Living
The role of "helper" and "servant" is not weak or less valued in God's view of reality. God deeply values what you do to encourage, to lift up, and to support those around you. Shine with radiance in the darkness.

SERVICE AS A LIFESTYLE

In Romans 16:1 Paul used the Greek word *diakonos* to describe Phoebe's ministry in the church. This word, translated "servant," can also refer to the role of deacon or deaconess within the church. While Phoebe likely served in some official capacity within the church at Cenchrea, but clearly *diakonos* or servanthood was far more than a role for Phoebe—she had positive effects on everyone around her. Paul didn't highly praise Phoebe because of her servant role in the church, but rather because helping and serving others was a lifestyle!

6. Imagine that you want to plant a new church in a diverse community that is hostile to the values of Jesus Christ. Describe the possible results of assigning a new church leader who does not have a servant's heart.

7. Think of someone who you believe lives out Phoebe's example of servanthood. What do that individual's words and actions tell you about his or her beliefs?

Principle for Living

In our "me-first" world, servant hearts are powerful tools for transformation. Whatever you lovingly do to serve within your church will strengthen the body of believers and attract others through your active love to Jesus.

EMBRACING THE TRUTH
20-25 Minutes

LEADER: This section focuses on helping group members integrate what they've learned from the Bible into their own hearts and lives. Invite volunteers to read the Bible passages.

BECOMING A SUPER-SERVANT

Our culture often expects us to be superwomen: we ladies can do it all, have it all, juggle it all, and keep it all together. But how many of us are wearing out under the strain of such unrealistic expectations? Maybe you're thinking as you read about Phoebe, "*Sure, Phoebe could worry about everyone else's needs. She was a saint. Maybe not even a wife or mother. Try being a servant when no one appreciates all you're carrying. Try being a servant when you're pulled in 100 different directions!*"

1. In what ways do you feel the pressure of being Superwoman? What do you see as the difference between striving to be a superwoman and practicing servanthood as a lifestyle?

The Bible tells us that true fulfillment is a blessing given not to superwomen, but to faithful servants (Matthew 25:21). That means there's hope for all of us! We don't have to overextend ourselves to be the best wives, mothers, employees, friends, neighbors, and interior decorators. Instead, we can find purpose and joy through simple acts of service that tell others, "I care about you just as much as I care about me." That is the basis of true fulfillment.

Perhaps we can better understand what inspired Phoebe's servant attitude and find a greater desire to approach life with our own by studying Phoebe's greatest inspirational teacher, Jesus Christ.

¹ Before the Passover Festival, Jesus knew that His hour had come to depart from this world to the Father. Having loved His own who were in the world, He loved them to the end. ... ³ Jesus knew that the Father had given everything into His hands, that He had come from God, and that He was going back to God. ⁴ So He got up from supper, laid aside His robe, took a towel, and tied it around Himself. ⁵ Next, He poured water into a basin and began to wash His disciples' feet and to dry them with the towel tied around Him.

JOHN 13:1,3-5, HCSB

2. According to John 13, what motivated and enabled Jesus' servant attitude?

²⁵ Jesus called [the disciples] over and said, "You know that the rulers of the Gentiles dominate them, and the men of high position exercise power over them. ²⁶ It must not be like that among you. On the contrary, whoever wants to become great among you must be your servant, ²⁷ and whoever wants to be first among you must be your slave; ²⁸ just as the Son of Man did not come to be served, but to serve, and to give His life—a ransom for many."

MATTHEW 20:25-28, HCSB

3. Compare and contrast Jesus' idea of leadership with the other models of leadership that you have seen or experienced.

⁵ Make your own attitude that of Christ Jesus, ⁶ who, existing in the form of God, did not consider equality with God as something to be used for His own advantage. ⁷ Instead He emptied Himself by assuming the form of a slave, taking on the likeness of men. And when He had come as a man in His external form, ⁸ He humbled Himself by becoming obedient to the point of death—even to death on a cross.

PHILIPPIANS 2:5-8, HCSB

4. What are the characteristics of a servant attitude you see highlighted in Philippians 2:5-8 and evident in the life of Jesus? Which of these would you like to develop more in your life?

5. Describe a time when you found it difficult to be a servant in actions or in attitude. Why do you think Jesus asks you to be a servant anyway?

6. What have you learned from one of the more challenging instances of servanthood?

Principle for Living

God wants to fulfill the deepest desires of your heart and only He knows the path that will lead to lasting happiness and fulfillment.
It won't come from chasing after your own comforts and gratification, but only as you rest in the arms of God and lay down your life to serve God and others.

CONNECTING - *10-15 Minutes*

LEADER: Use "Connecting" as a time to continue encouraging and supporting one another as you examine the thoughts, motives, and attitudes of your hearts. Invite everyone to join in the discussions.

OVERFLOW FROM THE HEART

You may feel that you do your fair share of serving. You keep your family's laundry cleaned and put away. You feed, bathe, and play with your children. You turn in your work at the office prior to deadline. You help out at church. Yet, too often your heart's attitude may be anything but humility, affection, and others-focused. Serving others willingly may *not* be something that comes naturally, but it *is* something that can be sparked supernaturally as you allow the Spirit of Jesus to fill you.

LEADER INSTRUCTIONS FOR THE GROUP EXPERIENCE: Before the meeting begins, set up a DVD player. Be sure to bring a DVD of the film, A Walk to Remember, *which stars Shane West and Mandy Moore (2002). Read the following paragraph to set up the clip, and then show from the end of Scene 26 "Father and son" through the beginning of Scene 28 "Her miracle" (1:29:28 to 1:35:02 on the DVD timer). Discuss the questions after viewing the scene.*

In the movie *A Walk to Remember*, reckless and arrogant Landon Carter (West) is skating through high school on his looks and bravado. Landon's life is turned upside down when events thrust him into the world of Jaimie Sullivan (Moore). Jaimie is an unfashionable preacher's kid whose self-confidence doesn't depend on the opinions of others. On a journey he never expected, Brandon is deeply changed through Jamie's faith, authenticity, and servanthood. Along the way, the two fall in love. The problem is that Jaimie is dying of an incurable disease.

When Jaime has to be hospitalized with her illness, the roles reverse and Landon becomes the one who serves Jaimie. Landon discovers that Jaimie is enamored with stars and planets and hopes to build a very large telescope to see a comet that's passing by earth soon. Because Jaimie is ill, Brandon decides to work hard to build the telescope in time for her to see the comet.

1. What do you think Brandon hoped to gain by building the telescope for Jaimie? Why do you think he proposed marriage knowing she only had a short time to live?

2. In the end, what did Brandon gain through serving Jaimie? What did he have to sacrifice?

3. Why do you think heart motivation is so crucial to our acts of service?

A few years after Jaimie's death, her father comments that Brandon had been the fulfillment of Jaimie's life ambition: "to see a miracle." Heartfelt compassion and a desire to serve dramatically change the lives of everyone who had been involved with the couple.

ALTERNATIVE GROUP EXPERIENCE: An alternative to using the scene from **A Walk to Remember** *is to read or listen to the moving resignation speech of Robertson McQuilken as president of Columbia International University. As a group, discuss this powerful story of love and sacrifice that's chronicled in a book entitled* **A Promise Kept.** *The speech is also recorded on* **A Promise Kept Audio CD** *available at www.familylife.com.*

4. If you knew that this was the last year of your life, what good works would you want to accomplish? What regrets would you have over things you neglected to do?

5. At your funeral, what do you want people to say about your influence on their lives? How do you think your life story would change if you abandoned yourself to playing a larger servant role in God's great story of redemption?

Share prayer requests that you will pray over between now and the next session. In addition, pray that God will enable each group member to rediscover a heart of compassion this week.

PRAYER REQUESTS:

TAKING IT HOME

LEADER: Encourage each person to set aside quiet time this week, so she can make the most of this group experience. Continue to highlight the importance of writing down thoughts, feelings, and key insights that God reveals.

QUESTIONS TO TAKE TO MY HEART

The following questions ask you to look into your heart and focus on your deepest feelings about yourself. Your behavior—not your intellectual stance—is the best indicator of your truest beliefs in your innermost being (Psalm 51:6, NASB). This is spiritual introspection time; look deep into the underlying beliefs down in your heart where your truest attitudes and motivations live.

❧ *As I look at my own service, am I helping others out of some rigid view of duty or with genuine care that radiates from the love I'm receiving from God?*

❧ *What in my attitude or habits would have to change in order for me to truly embody a servant attitude? What concerns or other priorities hold me back from living my life in such a way that my life will have an eternal impact on others?*

A QUESTION TO TAKE TO GOD

When you ask God a question, expect His Spirit to guide your heart to discover His truth. Be careful not to rush or manufacture an answer. Don't write down what you think the "right answer" is. Don't turn the Bible into a spiritual reference book or encyclopedia. Just pose a question to God and wait on Him. Remember, the litmus test for anything we hear from God is alignment with the Bible as our ultimate truth source. Keep a journal of the insights you gain from your time with God.

❧ *At the end of my life, I long to walk into Your arms, God, and hear You say, "Well done, good and faithful servant!" In what areas am I overextending beyond what You want for my service, trying to be Superwoman?*

❧ *What is Your heart's desire for my life as I move ahead from here?*

SCRIPTURE NOTES

Session Three

ROMANS 16:1-2

16:1-2 I commend ... Phoebe. It is likely that Phoebe carried Paul's letter from Corinth to the church at Rome. Typical in letters of his day, Paul includes a note of commendation in which he makes two requests: that they receive Phoebe as a sister in the Lord, and that they assist her because she has helped many others. *Phoebe* was probably a woman of wealth and influence who had given herself for God's kingdom. Phoebe. Her name, which means "radiant," originally referred to Apollo, whose symbol was usually some form of light. But after her new birth in Christ, Phoebe's life reflected the radiant joy and love of Jesus. Psalm 34:4-5 reads, *I sought the LORD, and He answered me and delivered me from all my fears. Those who look to Him are radiant with joy; their faces will never be ashamed.* And the author of Ephesians tells us in Ephesians 5:27 that through Christ's love and sacrifice, the Church — made up of sinful, imperfect people — is transformed into a *radiant church, without stain or wrinkle or any other blemish, but holy and blameless.* (NIV)

16:2 great help. The word "help" or "benefactor" in the Greek is *prostatis,* "a word used in classical Greek of trainers who dedicated themselves to assist an athlete competing for a prize." (Richards, *Women of the Bible,* p. 154.)

EPHESIANS 4:18-19

4:18 hardness of their hearts. The center of their being (the heart) has become "stone-like" or "petrified."

4:19 promiscuity ... impurity ... desire. By these three nouns, Paul describes those things into which pagan life has evolved.

JOHN 13:1-5

13:1 Jesus knew. Here in verses 3 and 11, John emphasizes what Jesus knew. This stresses the fact that Jesus was in charge of the events leading to His death (10:18).

13:3 Jesus' self-knowledge was at the heart of His willingness and ability to serve. This verse says that He knew who He was in terms of where He had come from (the Father), where He was going (back to the Father), and what His role was while He was here.

13:4-5 to wash His disciples' feet. Normally people's dusty, sandaled feet were washed by the lowest-ranking servant of the household before a meal was served. Jesus' action was deliberate. Removing His outer clothing was a sign He was going to do some work, and it would have identified Him with a servant who generally worked in minimal garb. The other Gospels mention that at the Last Supper there was a discussion among the Twelve about who was the greatest (Luke 22:24). In that context, Jesus identified the greatest as the one who was the servant (Luke 22:25-26).

MATTHEW 20:25-28

20:24 they became indignant. All 12 share the view that the kingdom will be earthly and political, with Jesus as the reigning king and them as His chief lieutenants.

20:26 servant. Rather than become masters (and exercise authority), they are to become servants (and meet the needs of others).

20:28 ransom. "Ransom" was a word used generally to describe the act of freeing people from bondage, whether through the literal payment of a purchase price or through some act of deliverance.

PHILIPPIANS 2:5-8

2:6 existing. This word carries the idea of pre-existence. By using it, Paul is saying Jesus always existed in the form of God. *the form of God.* The Greek word here is *morphe* (used twice by Paul in this passage). He says that Jesus was in His nature (form) God, but that He then took upon Himself the form or nature of a slave (v. 7). This is a key word in understanding the nature of Christ. He possessed the complete, essential nature of God. *to be used for His own advantage.* Jesus did not have to "snatch" equality with God. It was His already, and He could give it away.

2:7 emptied Himself. Literally, "to empty," or "to pour out until the container is empty." *assuming the form of a slave.* From being the ultimate master, He became the lowest servant. *taking on.* In contrast to the verb in verse 6 (which stresses

Christ's eternal nature), this verb points to the fact that at a particular time He was born in the likeness of a human being. *the likeness of men.* The point is not that Jesus just seemed to be human. He assumed the identity of a person and was in actuality a human being.

2:8 He humbled Himself. Jesus is the ultimate model of One who lived a life of self-sacrifice, self-renunciation, and self-surrender. *obedient to the point of death.* The extent of this humbling is defined by this clause. Jesus humbled Himself to the furthest point one can go. He submitted to death itself for the sake of humanity. *death on a cross.* Crucifixion was a harsh, demeaning, and utterly painful way to die. According to the Old Testament, those who died by hanging on a tree were considered to have been cursed by God.

SESSION QUOTATIONS

1 Sue Poorman Richards and Lawrence O. Richards, *Women of the Bible*, (Nashville, TN: Thomas Nelson, 2003), p. 154.

PRISCILLA: LIVING ON THE EDGE

Imagine the government sends a nation-wide notice: "All Christians must vacate the country within 30 days." What would you do in the face of such a decree? How would you respond to its demands? Where would you go? Do you think the experience would tempt you to renounce your faith or would it make you more determined to live it? This scenario is not far from the reality that met Priscilla and her husband, Aquila, in the years following Christ's resurrection.

BREAKING THE ICE - *10-15 Minutes*

LEADER: These "Breaking the Ice" questions encourage group members to share a little more about their stories and personal bents. Set the tone by giving your responses first. Watch the time.

1. On the following risk scale, how much of a risk taker are you? What life experiences have shaped your response to risk?

   1   2   3   4   5   6   7   8   9   10

   Predictability and   I love adventure and
   safety are vital to me   my life is an adventure!

2. Describe the riskiest thing you have done. How does risk-taking make you feel?

3. If you were forced to leave your home because of religious persecution, what practical things could you do to turn it into a positive instead of a negative experience?

LEADER: Encourage the group to share insights from the "Taking It Home" questions. This should only take a couple of minutes but allow more time if someone has a unique insight or needs the support of the group.

4. As you spent time with God this week, what did you discover about the attitudes of your heart when it comes to serving others? In what areas did God rearrange your priorities?

DISCOVERING THE TRUTH
25-30 Minutes

LEADER: Invite various group members to read the Bible passages aloud. Your group should be gelling well now and enjoying discussions. Be sure to leave time for the "Embracing the Truth" and "Connecting" segments.

MAKING THE BEST OF HARD TIMES

In Acts 18:1-4, we learn that the anti-Semitic Emperor Claudius recently exiled the Jews from Italy, among them Aquila and Priscilla.

¹ After Athens, Paul went to Corinth. ² That is where he discovered Aquila, a Jew born in Pontus, and his wife, Priscilla. They had just arrived from Italy, part of the general expulsion of Jews from Rome ordered by Claudius. ³ Paul moved in with them, and they worked together at their common trade of tentmaking.

ACTS 18:1-3, THE MESSAGE

[Paul] stayed there a year and six months, teaching the word of God among them.

ACTS 18:11, HCSB

1. What kind of relationship do you suppose Priscilla and her husband developed with Paul during the 18 months they were together in Corinth?

2. How did the couple make the best of their banishment as they found new opportunities to serve God? In what ways did God use this situation to further His mission in Corinth?

18 So Paul, having stayed on for many days, said good-bye to the brothers and sailed away to Syria. Priscilla and Aquila were with him.

ACTS 18:18A, HCSB

19 The churches of the Asian province greet you. Aquila and Priscilla greet you heartily in the Lord, along with the church that meets in their home.

1 CORINTHIANS 16:19, HCSB

3. How did all of the knowledge Priscilla and Aquila gained while Paul stayed in their home transform their lives and work for the Lord?

4. Having lost one home to exile, Priscilla and Aquila seem surprisingly willing to give up their Corinthian home to continue missionary work with Paul. Why do you think Priscilla and her husband were so quick to accept the opportunity to serve as missionaries?

How do Priscilla and Aquila demonstrate a "journey" mentality rather than a "destination" mentality in the way they live their lives?

Paul worked together with Priscilla and Aquila to establish the church Corinth, an influential commercial city in Greece. They then traveled gether to Syria to spread the gospel of Jesus there.

Principle of Living

When you face hard times, remember that God has great things in store for you. By choosing to view life as a journey or an adventure to be lived to the fullest rather than as a destination to be achieved, you'll open yourself to being used in surprising ways in God's great life-giving mission.

Despite difficult times and numerous risks, Priscilla and Aquila's open-nded, open-hearted approach allowed God a wonderful opportunity to e their lives in new and exciting ways. Their trust in the goodness of God's art made them even more adaptable to new situations and more attentive God's direction. It made them more valuable to the Kingdom of God.

IVING BEYOND YOURSELF

iscilla and Aquila did not pursue knowledge for knowledge's sake or st to deepen their own marital or spiritual lives. Their goal was life-nsforming pursuits for themselves and life-giving service to the people ound them.

4 Jew named Apollos, a native Alexandrian, an eloquent man who was powerful in Scriptures, arrived in Ephesus. [25] This man had been instructed in the way of the rd; and being fervent in spirit, he spoke and taught the things about Jesus accurately, though he knew only John's baptism. [26] He began to speak boldly in the synagogue. ter Priscilla and Aquila heard him, they took him home and explained the way of God him more accurately. [27] When he wanted to cross over to Achaia, the brothers wrote to disciples urging them to welcome him. After he arrived, he greatly helped those who believed through grace. [28] For he vigorously refuted the Jews in public, demonstrating rough the Scriptures that Jesus is the Messiah.

ACTS 18:24-28, HCSB

6. Apollos was a naturally gifted speaker and teacher. What dangers could arise in the church if someone teaches without having a full understanding of Scripture and a growing experience of God?

7. What's the significance of the Priscilla and Aquila taking Apollos into their home? What did the couple risk by taking in Apollos?

8. What can we learn from Priscilla and Aquila's willingness to teach and invest in the lives of others? How should their example impact the way we interact with people?

The early church faced serious opposition from a hostile, pagan culture and persecution from an oppressive government. The young church desperately needed to maintain unity to display Christ's love to the world and to support one another in the face of crises. Priscilla and Aquila used their knowledge of the Scriptures and of Jesus, gleaned through personal study and through their time with Paul, to sharpen Apollos' faith and message. In so doing, they added weight and validity to his message and expanded the impact he carried forward into the lives of so many.

Principle of Living
Accept difficulties as opportunities to learn more about God and about yourself.
As you deepen your trust in God, He will deepen your understanding
of His heart and His ways and,
He will equip you to take the message of life — life in Jesus — to others.

Embracing the Truth
10-15 Minutes

LEADER: This section continues the discussion of living the adventure as we join Jesus in His mission of healing, freedom, and redemption. Strive to help group members integrate what they've learned from the Bible into their own hearts and lives.

LIVING THE ADVENTURE

After their exile from Rome and time in Corinth (Greece), Priscilla and Aquila help Paul plant a thriving church in Syria as well. After years of hosting and equipping the church in Ephesus, a thriving port city in Syria (modern-day Turkey), Priscilla and Aquila eventually returned to Rome. In his letter to the church in Rome, Paul commends them highly, highlighting the tremendous impact this couple created as partners in his mission to the Gentiles.

⁵ Give my greetings to Prisca and Aquila, my co-workers in Christ Jesus, ⁴ who risked their own necks for my life. Not only do I thank them, but also so do all the Gentile churches. ⁵ Greet also the church that meets in their home.

ROMANS 16:3-5, HCSB

²³ During that time [in Ephesus where Priscilla and Aquila hosted the church] there was a major disturbance about the Way [a name given the Christian movement]. ... ²⁸ they were filled with rage ... ²⁹ So the city was filled with confusion; and they rushed all together into the amphitheater, dragging along Gaius and Aristarchus, Macedonians who were Paul's traveling companions. ³⁰ Though Paul wanted to go in before the people, the disciples did not let him.

ACTS 19:23,28-30, HCSB

1. What kind of person would you imagine Priscilla must have been in order to work alongside Paul in planting churches and then hosting those churches in her large homes?

Session Four

2. Note the tone of Paul's greeting and commendation as he refers to Priscilla by her nickname. How does Paul feel about this woman and her husband? What stands out in his mind as he mentions them?

3. It's likely this couple risked their lives (Romans 16:4) to save Paul during the riot noted in Acts 19. As you've traced Priscilla's life, in what ways would you say she had a "reckless faith"? How reckless is your faith?

Principle for Living

People like Priscilla and Aquila helped "turn the world upside down" (Acts 17:6).
As you encounter God, you'll never be the same.
As you begin to step outside your comfort zone, Jesus will take you
on an adventure that will rock our world in ways you never imagined.

We all experience difficulties and life upheavals. In that way, we can all relate with Priscilla's story. The point of challenges is not to break us or even to make us stronger. As we trust Him, God will use life's challenges as opportunities to reshape us, to stretch us, to make us more dependent on the God we serve, and to give us a larger role in His story of redemption.

4. Recall a challenge or heartbreak you or your family have faced. How has God redeemed that difficulty, bringing something good out of something bad?

5. What difficult life lessons have your struggles taught you that can serve as life lessons to pass on to others about God? About life?

CONNECTING *-15-20 Minutes*

LEADER: Use the "Connecting" experience to help group members connect their hearts with the heart of God. Encourage and pport one another as you face struggles on your journeys. Set the tone for enness by sharing your story first.

or some, living in Priscilla's shoes would have been exciting, while for hers it would have been frightening. But no matter what our risk-taking aracteristics, we must consider that anything worthwhile in life requires k and trade-offs.

HE DILEMMA OF RISK

ADER INSTRUCTIONS FOR THE GROUP EXPERIENCE: Before e meeting begins, set up a DVD player. Be sure to bring a DVD of the film, pider-Man 2, which stars Tobey Maguire and Kirsten Dunst (2004). First, ad the following paragraph to set up the FIRST clip. Then show Scene 48 "Web ve" (1:52:59 to 1:55:18 on the DVD timer). Discuss question 1 after viewing e first clip.

In the movie *Spider-Man 2*, Mary Jane Watson (Dunst) has been best ends for years with Peter Parker (Maguire). She has always hoped for omantic relationship, but Peter has let her down time and again. Peter's cret life as Spider-Man pulls him in two directions at once. Finally, M.J. eets another wonderful man and plans to marry him. M.J. finally discovers ter's secret when he rescues her from deadly peril. He explains their lemma in Scene 48.

Why couldn't Mary Jane and Peter be together? How do you think she felt as she resigned herself to the path of security and comfort?

ADER INSTRUCTIONS FOR THE GROUP EXPERIENCE: It's time to ow the SECOND clip from Spider-Man 2. Show Scenes 50 "Here Comes the ide" and 51 "The Final Swing," which ends the movie (1:57:99 to 2:02:30 on e DVD timer). Discuss the remaining questions.

Session Four

2. Why do we cheer about Mary Jane's choice in the end even though she leaves her fiancé standing at the altar?

3. Mary Jane says, "I know there'll be risks, but I will face them with you." What risks will she have to face? What trade-offs and losses did she have to consider in her decision to follow her heart?

4. Mary Jane also says, "I can't survive without you. ... It's wrong that we should only be half alive." What did she mean by this? What was it that she wanted so much that she was willing to risk it all?

5. What do you think M.J. was thinking and feeling as she stood at the window in the closing shot of the movie? What are some risks or challenges with which you've been struggling in your own faith journey?

Share prayer requests that you will pray over between now and the next session. Also pray together today, asking God to help each woman as she wrestles with living from her heart and stepping out of her comfort zone to joining God in the grand adventure. Pray also that the married women will develop the level of unity and teamwork with their husbands that Priscilla strived to create with Aquila.

PRAYER REQUESTS:

TAKING IT HOME

LEADER: "Taking It Home" this week highlights reckless faith, reawakening our hearts, and living with a journey mentality. Encourage each person to find a unique setting for her quiet time this week. Instruct group members to choose a location (possibly in picturesque outside spot) that will help her to step outside her comfort zone. Encourage group members to develop a habit of keeping a journal.

A QUESTION TO TAKE TO MY HEART

The following question asks you to look into your heart and focus on your deepest feelings about yourself. Our behaviors are the best indicators of what we really believe deep down. Look deep into the underlying beliefs down in your heart where your truest attitudes and motivations live. Spend some time reflecting.

❧ *What's really holding me back from giving all that I have and all that I am to God? What fears am I carrying in my heart of hearts that prevents me from abandoning myself to God and living with a more reckless faith?*

QUESTIONS TO TAKE TO GOD

When you ask God a question, expect His Spirit to guide your heart to discover His truth. Be careful not to rush or manufacture an answer. Don't write down what you think the "right answer" is. Don't turn the Bible into a spiritual reference book or encyclopedia. Just pose a question to God and wait on Him. Remember, the litmus test for anything we hear from God is alignment with the Bible as our ultimate truth source. Keep a journal of the insights you gain from your time with God.

In The Journey of Desire, *John Eldredge writes: "Bringing our heart along in our life's journey is the most important mission of our lives—and the hardest. It all turns on what we do with our desire. If you will look around, you will see that most people have abandoned the journey. They have lost heart. They have camped in places of resignation or indulgence, or trapped in prisons of despair."*

God, in what areas of my life have I camped out in places of resignation or indulgence? Where did I abandon the journey or lose heart? What do You want to say to me about where I am right now on the journey?

Scripture Notes

ACTS 18:1-3, 18, 24-28

18:1 The next stop for Paul on his second missionary journey was Corinth, a prosperous seaport 50 miles from Athens.

18:2 Aquila … Priscilla. Aquila meant "Eagle," and Priscilla meant something like "Wise Woman." This couple apparently converted in Rome prior to meeting Paul. They became important co-workers with him.

general expulsion of Jews from Rome ordered by Claudius. Because of uprisings in the Jewish community at Rome due to the influence of a man named Chrestus, riots broke out among the Roman Jews between those who believed in Jesus as the Messiah and those who did not. To solve the problem, the emperor simply ordered all Jews to leave! While the expulsion order was not strictly enforced, for a time the Jews were forbidden to meet, which led many to leave anyway.

18:18 Priscilla and Aquila were with him. It is significant that Priscilla's name is mentioned first, ahead of her husband (Rom. 16:3; 2 Tim. 4:19). This was rarely done and may indicate that Priscilla was the more outspoken of the two. Passages that introduce the couple formally or officially name Aquila first as the head of his household (Acts 18:2; 1 Cor. 16:19).

He shaved his head … because he had taken a vow. Pious Jews would take vows, based on the pattern of the Nazarites (Num. 6:1-21), as an indication of their devotion to God. Since the cutting of one's hair indicated the termination of the vow, Paul may have made a vow of dedication to God for as long as he was in Corinth in gratefulness to God's promise of protection (v. 10). While normally vows would be terminated by shaving one's head and offering a sacrifice in the temple at Jerusalem, people far from the city could shave their heads where they were and carry the trimmings to the temple to be presented along with a sacrifice at that time. Luke may have included this incident as evidence that Paul did not abandon the traditions of his people

18:25 While Apollos was an earnest, articulate believer in Jesus, he had not received the whole story of the gospel. Just what he was lacking is unclear, but, as the story in 19:1-7 indicates, he may not have heard of the coming of the Holy Spirit promised to those who are baptized in the name of Jesus.

CORINTHIANS 16:19

church ... in their home. From its
...eption, the Ephesian church served
...he focal point for outreach into
...province of Asia (Acts 19:1-10).
...impossible to know how much
... role in its success Aquila and
...scilla played, but Paul clearly
...sidered them invaluable co-workers
...preading the gospel (Rom. 16:3-
...Chronologically, this reference
...cedes Romans 16:3-5.

...MANS 16:3-6

...the church ... in their home. During
...first two centuries, there were no
...cial church buildings, so Christians
...: in the homes of their members (1
...r. 16:19; Col. 4:15; Philemon. 2).
...e growth of these churches was
...rwhelming. Priscilla and Aquila,
...l the other church hosts, had to
...wealthy owners of large homes
...o generously used their resources
...dvance God's kingdom. Priscilla
...l Aquila relocated frequently. This
...s not rare among first-century
...inesspeople. Aquila was from
...tus in northern Asia Minor, but
...irst appeared in Acts moving from
...ne to Corinth (Acts 18:2). He and
...scilla relocated to Ephesus and
...ted the church there (1 Cor. 16:19).
...nans 16:5 indicates they were back
...Rome and hosting that church. By
...end of Paul's life, they were living
...phesus again (2 Tim. 4:19).

SESSION QUOTATIONS

1 John Eldredge, *The Journey of Desire*,
  (Nashville: Thomas Nelson, 2000),
  pp. 14-15.

Session Four

JUNIA: BECOMING AN OUTSTANDING CHARACTER

Most of us either laugh or cringe when flipping through an old high school annual or yearbook. The section reserved for superlative awards is most likely to bring a strong response. Superlatives are given to those high school seniors who are supposedly "outstanding" in some particular way; maybe Joe received the certificate for being "Best Dressed" and Susan was awarded the title, "Most Likely to Succeed." Superlatives are handed out so that everyone will remember their recipients as special, and perhaps even to subtly encourage others to compare themselves to the winners.

In this session, we'll discuss a husband and wife team, Andronicus and Junia, whom Paul labeled with a unique superlative title. "Outstanding Character" truly defined this couple who left behind a faith example we are all wise to emulate.

BREAKING THE ICE - *5-10 Minutes*

LEADER: These "Breaking the Ice" questions are designed to get people talking. Encourage each group member to participate, but be sure to keep things moving.

1. Your life can be read like a letter sent to the world. What kind of letter have you been this week? This year?
   - ◯ Complaint letter
   - ◯ Business letter
   - ◯ Impersonal text message
   - ◯ Blank page
   - ◯ Love letter
   - ◯ Letter of encouragement
   - ◯ Other: _____

   Explain your answer.

Session Five

2. Which of the following superlative awards would you be most likely to receive this week?

○ Most Punctual
○ Best Housekeeper
○ Most Dedicated Employee
○ Happiest Person in the House
○ Best All Around
○ Most Likely to Do Better Next Week
○ Other: _____

LEADER: Encourage the group to share insights from the "Taking It Home" questions. This should only take a couple of minutes but allow more time if someone has a unique insight or needs the support of the group.

3. What did you hear from God this week? Did you find places where you have camped out in resignation or indulgence? What barriers in your life or your beliefs keep you from living from your heart?

DISCOVERING THE TRUTH
15-20 Minutes

LEADER: "Discovering the Truth" will explore some outstanding character traits of Junia. Invite various group members to read the Bible passages. Leave ample time for "Embracing the Truth" and "Connecting."

MOST LIKELY TO STAND OUT

Throughout his stay in prison, Paul wrote many letters to build up the church, to strengthen people in the faith, and to encourage and greet his many friends in the Lord. While Paul made mention of dozens of specific people, the exhortation he reserved for Junia and her husband, Andronicus, was especially uplifting. From it we can gain clues into the kind of Christ-followers we should all strive to become.

Session Five

Greet Andronicus and Junia, my fellow countrymen and fellow prisoners. They are outstanding among the apostles, and they were also in Christ before me.

ROMANS 16:7, HCSB

LEADER: Discuss as many discovery questions as time permits. Encourage participation by inviting different individuals to respond. It will help to highlight in advance the questions you don't want to miss. Be familiar with the Scripture Notes at the end of this session.

Romans 16:7 is the only verse in all of Scripture that mentions Andronicus or Junia, and yet they may well have received the Apostle Paul's highest commendation.

1. How would you define "outstanding" in your own words? What would someone have to demonstrate in order for you to believe he or she has an "outstanding" relationship with Jesus?

2. Notice that "they" are outstanding. Andronicus and Junia come together as a package deal. How can a strong, vibrant couple contribute to the health of the church and the cause of Christ?

3. Paul is proud of his kinship with Andronicus and Junia; he was equally as proud of his shared prison time with this couple. Why do you think both husband and wife were imprisoned with Paul?

It's fascinating that Junia was in prison along with the men. Paul was often imprisoned for his bold activities in sharing the gospel of grace and hope in Jesus the promised Messiah. Junia must have been very active in this vital work of sharing the good news of Jesus death and resurrection with the Gentiles. She also must have just as bold and courageous as Paul.

4. What do you think Paul meant when he said that Andronicus and Junia were "in Christ before him?" How might their example have shaped Paul's life?

Junia and Andronicus were long-time followers of Jesus. Perhaps they had even spoken with Jesus first-hand. Clearly they were changed by their personal experience with the resurrected Savior. Their courageous faith and character had an impact on the passionate young Pharisee who would one day become the most influential evangelist in Christian history.

5. Junia and Andronicus lived out dynamic witness for Christ, a witness that church leaders found remarkable. What do you think it takes to be an "outstanding" ambassador or witness for Christ?

Often persecuted and even killed for their faith, apostles were those who had seen the risen Christ and spread the message of Jesus to the ends of the earth. While we know little about Junia and her husband, the apostles knew them well.

Junia and Andronicus were surely people of integrity and character. Their lives were so full of love for Christ and His message that it spilled out into their actions and words. People could recognize Jesus by looking at their lives. Their values actions flowed from their consistent walk with the Lord, a fact not lost on those who came in contact with them.

Principle for Living
Living with integrity means that your actions align with what you say you believe. Outstanding moral character and Christian testimony are rooted in Jesus Christ. When your values and actions flow from a consistent and dynamic walk with Jesus, you are on your way to becoming an "outstanding" representative for Him.

EMBRACING THE TRUTH
25-30 Minutes

LEADER: This section will help group members integrate what they've learned from the life of Junia about character and living with fruitfulness into their own lives. Invite volunteers to read the Bible passages.

A FRUITFUL CONNECTION

Modern society's version of a fruitful life is one filled with things, cash, titles, and fame. But in God's economy a fruitful life does not consist of things but in the quality of our relationships with Jesus and with others. In John 15, Jesus used a beautiful word picture to illustrate this idea to His disciples and also to us.

⁵ I am the vine; you are the branches. The one who remains in Me and I in him produces much fruit, because you can do nothing without Me. ⁶ If anyone does not remain in Me, he is thrown aside like a branch and he withers. They gather them, throw them into the fire, and they are burned. ⁷ If you remain in Me and My words remain in you, ask whatever you want and it will be done for you. ⁸ My Father is glorified by this: that you produce much fruit and prove to be My disciples.

JOHN 15:5-8, HCSB

1. How does being connected to a vine contribute to a branch's fruitfulness (verse 5)? Why do we find it so difficult to stay closely connected to the true Vine?

2. Jesus is commissioning us to "produce much fruit" (verse 8) — eternal fruit in our own lives, but even more so fruit that has eternal significance in the lives of others. What are some ways we can be fruit producers?

A FRUITFUL SACRIFICE

It sounds so pleasant and easy: remain in Jesus and you will have a fruitful life, but we know it's not. As Junia curled up in her dark prison cell to sleep,

Session Five

she say to herself, "*This remaining-in-Jesus thing is a piece of cake*"? Not ely. Jesus did not promise us an easy life; in fact, if we are as committed knowing and serving God as Junia did, we will spend our lives facing llenges, heartbreaks, and the constant struggle to overcome our own nplacency. In his book *Shattered Dreams*, Larry Crabb discusses this uggle: "The search to discover God requires that we abandon ourselves, t we give up control of what matters most, and that we place our *confidence* Someone we cannot manage." [1] Paul states the same concept this way ...

have been crucified with Christ; [20] *and I no longer live, but Christ lives in me. e life I now live in the flesh, I live by faith in the Son of God, who loved me) gave Himself for me.*

GALATIANS 2:19B-20, HCSB

Why do you think people often struggle with the idea of abandoning their lives to God and His will? What core belief is behind these issues?

What was Paul's motivation to abandon his old life and desires in exchange for his new life in Christ (verse 20 and 2 Corinthians 5:15-19)?

Describe the character of someone in whom Christ obviously dwells. What attitudes suggest that someone is living not for Christ but for self?

Principle for Living

art from the life of Christ within you, you can do nothing of eternal value. You will ly live in Christ and He in you if you trust Him and love Him who gave everything had to reconcile your broken relationship and redeem your life now and for eternity.

A FRUITFUL PERSPECTIVE

A fruitful life is also a faithful one that's productive for the Kingdom of God. Junia and Andronicus were rightly focused on the rewards in the eternal Kingdom of God rather than on the rewards of this life. They embraced Jesus' perspective just as Paul did.

[Jesus said:] ²⁵ For whoever wants to save his life will lose it, but whoever loses his life for me will find it. ²⁶ What good will it be for a man if he gains the whole world, yet forfeits his soul? Or what can a man give in exchange for his soul? ²⁷ For the Son of Man is going to come in his Father's glory with his angels, and then he will reward each person according to what he has done.

MATTHEW 16:25-27, NIV

[Paul from prison:] ²¹ For to me, to live is Christ and to die is gain. ²² If I am to go on living in the body, this will mean fruitful labor for me.

PHILIPPIANS 1:21-22A, NIV

6. How does Jesus define a fruitful or outstanding life in Matthew 16:25-27? In what ways does our culture encourage us to save our lives and to live for our own gain?

7. What does it mean practically in our everyday lives to "lose our lives" for Christ or to say with Paul "For me, to live is Christ" (see Philippians 1:21-22)? In the context of all Jesus said and did, do you think this means that we should not enjoy this life?

8. When Jesus returns to establish His kingdom, for what does He promise to reward us? (*Note that Jesus repeats this again in John's vision of the future in Revelation 22:12.*) How does this affect the way you view your life?

In *The Journey of Desire*, John Eldredge highlights the dilemma of saving our lives to lose them: "Something awful has happened; something terrible. Something worse, even, than the fall of man. For in that greatest of all tragedies, we merely lost Paradise—and with it, everything that made life worth living. What has happened since is unthinkable: we've gotten used to it." [2]

Principle for Living
We so easily settle into this world as if it were our home.
But you were made for a life of eternity with Jesus. So, live focused on the
treasures and rewards of Heaven rather than the rewards of this world.

CONNECTING - *15-20 minutes*

LEADER: Use "Connecting" as a time to deepen relationships within the group and to help each woman connect with God in a more personal way. Encourage and support one another through the trying times of life. Be sensitive those who are dealing with difficult issues.

SHINING LIGHT

You cannot hide your character for long. Others see how you respond to the ups and downs of ordinary life. They see how you deal with death, taxes, dead batteries, strained relationships, priorities, finances, peer pressure, and temper tantrums. Others see your character, and they are influenced by it. Paul recognized that character is not a neutral quality. It is always a dynamic force, able to influence others toward or away from the heart of God.

² You yourselves are our letter, written in our hearts, known and read by everybody.
³ You should know that you are a letter from Christ, the result of our ministry, written not with ink but with the Spirit of the living God, not on tablets of stone but on tablets of human hearts.

2 CORINTHIANS 3:2-3, NIV

As our characters shine, whether with the light of Christ's love or with the green glow of ugly attitudes and sin, people will notice. In looking to verify our claims about Christ's love, they will read our lives.

1. How does it make you feel that your life and character is a letter "known and read by all men"? Describe a time when your behavior or attitude had a distinct influence on someone.

2. Which of life's challenges brings out the worst in you? What do you think your reaction to difficulties reveals about your relationship with God or the attitudes of your heart?

We are living letters of God's love, written to a lonely and loveless world. Our characters are a reflection of God's true nature and of God's true purpose for the world. There are people who will come to Christ, not because of philosophical debate or rational research, but because they see Jesus alive in us.

Principle for Living

Your character has an incredible power to shape the lives of others.
Others will either praise God because of your influence on their lives or form a negative opinion of Him based in part on your attitude.
Determine to shine positively for Christ; allow Him to live His life in and through you.

SELLING YOUR CHARACTER

LEADER INSTRUCTIONS FOR THE GROUP EXPERIENCE: Prior to meeting set up a DVD player and TV. Obtain the movie,* The Family Man, *starring Nicholas Cage (2001). Read the following paragraph to set up the scene and then show Scene 15 (1:38:34 to 1:40:00 on the DVD timer).

The Family Man tells the story of Jack Campbell, a successful business-man who wakes up to find himself living an alternate life—the life he gave up when he pursued success over life with his college sweetheart. Throughout the movie, Jack struggles between his desires for both worlds: the life of privilege and certainty or the life of love and meaning. Don Cheadle plays an unconventional angel who challenges Jack's assumptions about the meaning of life. In the scene we'll view, the angel uses a customer's willingness to sell her character as a powerful object lesson.

3. In the life Jack originally chose, he was willing to sell his character to make it big in New York. What did he learn about his choice by seeing a "glimpse" of what his life could have been?

4. What does the phrase "sell your character" mean to you? In what ways do you see people doing this?

5. What tempts us to sell our character? What lies must we believe in order to justify doing this?

6. Return to our earlier discussion in 2 Corinthians 3:2-3 about our lives as an open letter to the world. What message is God telling the world through your life? Is it a message of hope, of perseverance, of healing, of forgiveness, of inner peace, of new life, of grace? Explain.

Share prayer requests that you will pray over between now and the next session. In addition, pray that God will strengthen and encourage each participant as she takes her heart's questions to God this week.

PRAYER REQUESTS:

TAKING IT HOME

LEADER: *"Taking It Home" questions this week continue the discussion of character and the focus of our lives. Encourage each person to set aside quiet time this week, so she can make the most of this experience. Encourage each woman to focus on the positive ways that God has used her life thus far and that He has even more in store for her.*

QUESTIONS TO TAKE TO MY HEART

This is introspection time—time to grapple with what drives your thinking and behavior. Strive to understand what you really believe in your innermost being about God, yourself, and the world in which you live. Your behavior—not your intellectual stance—is the best indicator of your truest beliefs in your innermost being (Psalm 51:6, NASB).

✧ *What might God be doing through my life if I were to abandon myself completely to Him?*

✧ *Is the character I reveal to the world my authentic self? What needs to change in my life and in my relationship with God in order for me to develop an authentically godly character?*

Session Five

QUESTIONS TO TAKE TO GOD

hen you ask God a question, expect His Spirit to guide your heart to
cover His truth. Be careful not to rush or manufacture an answer.
n't write down what you think the "right answer" is. Don't turn the
le into a spiritual reference book or encyclopedia. Just pose a question
God and wait on Him. Remember, the litmus test for anything we
ar from God is alignment with the Bible as our ultimate truth source.
ep a journal of the insights you gain from your time with God.

*Jesus, what kind of letter have I been to the world?
What are You pleased about? Where do I need to change the story?*

*What does it mean to remain in You? What vision do You
have of my life if I lay myself completely in Your hands?*

Scripture Notes

JOHN 15:4-8

15:4 bear fruit. Although Paul uses the image of fruit to describe Christian character (Gal. 5:22-23), the fruit here probably relates to 4:35 and 12:24 where a similar agricultural image is used to speak of the many people who would come to Christ. Just as Jesus' fruitfulness was dependent on His doing the Father's will, so the disciple's is dependent on holding on to Jesus' teaching.

15:7 ask whatever you wish and it will be given you. Here the promise is in the context of spiritual fruitfulness. (See also its counterpart in verse 16.)

GALATIANS 2:19-20

2:20 I no longer live. Paul died in relationship to the Law. *Christ lives in me.* That which now activates the believer is the resurrection life and power of Jesus. *I live by faith.* Faith is that which bonds together the believer and the risen Christ. Paul will also refer to this as living by the Spirit (5:25).

PHILIPPIANS 1:21-22

1:21 to live is Christ. For Paul, his entire existence revolves around Christ. He is inspired by Christ; he works for Christ; his sole focus in life is Christ. He is a man with a single, all-consuming passion.

to die is gain. Death is the door into the presence of Christ. Death is not so much escape from hardship as it is entrance into joy.

SESSION QUOTATIONS:

1 Larry Crabb. *Shattered Dreams* (Colorado Springs, CO.: Waterbrook Press, 2001), p. 107.

2 John Eldredge, *The Journey of Desire*, (Nashville: Thomas Nelson, 2000), p. 9.

WOMEN OF HONOR: POINTING OTHERS TO THE LIGHT

Astronomer John Dobson dedicated his life to bringing the galaxies' wonders to the average person. In college Dobson became fascinated by stars and black holes and the worlds beyond. Out of this obsession, he built a portable telescope to set up on a San Francisco sidewalk. As it sat there, Dobson would call out to passers by, "Come, come see the sun!" Today thousands of amateur astronomers credit Dobson with their continuing fascination with the heavens. [1]

In our final session of *Held in High Esteem*, we'll focus on some early women who dedicated their lives to announcing, "Come, come see the Son!" The ladies Paul held in high regard longed to play a role in God's great redemptive story. Once they became new creations in Christ, their lives were marked by a steadfast and courageous faith in Jesus, a vision for bringing the Kingdom of God to earth, a servant attitude of humility, and dedication to building up other Christ-followers. As we discuss these ladies whom Paul highly esteemed, let's determine to follow their examples by allowing our lives to point others to Jesus, too.

BREAKING THE ICE - *10-15 Minutes*

LEADER INSTRUCTIONS FOR THE GROUP EXPERIENCE:
Bring in a variety of small household objects such as key chains, potholders, tape, flashlights, scissors, silverware, crystal creamers, spices, and candles. You might even ask participants to dig into their purses to contribute similar items to the collection.

1. Choose from the collection of household items one thing that you feel best represents your spiritual journey. Explain why you chose this.

2. Share one curious or new insight that God showed you about yourself, the kind of letter you've been to the world, or His vision for your life?

DISCOVERING THE TRUTH
25-30 Minutes

THE POWER OF A MENTION

Paul was a man who appreciated the men and women who served Christ alongside him. Through his letters we see that he recognized their individual worth, appreciated their unique value in Jesus' sight, and was determined to faithfully acknowledge their kingdom worth through his correspondence to the churches. While Paul sometimes included background information around the names of those he mentioned, as in the case of Priscilla, he more often named people in passing, as if their names alone told their stories. His greetings to Mary and Persis provide excellent examples.

Greet Mary, who has worked very hard for you. ... Greet my dear friend Persis, who has worked very hard in the Lord.

ROMANS 16:6,12, HCSB

1. Who comes to mind when you think of a church servant who works hard but never calls attention to herself? What do you notice about her attitude? What factors might motivate her service?

We know practically nothing about this woman, Mary, who shared one of the most common names of her day; however, Paul's notice of her suggests something special about her life. Mary did not just work hard, but very hard for the group of believers. She had an outstanding commitment to building up others in the faith, as did Persis. Persis was also a "dear friend."

Mary and Persis represent all those precious women in the church who never call attention to themselves, who might never serve in positions of leadership, who will never be noticed for their shining spiritual gifts, but who work hard through prayer, service, diligence, and sometimes long hours to keep the church focused and effective in its mission.

LEADER: Encourage participation by inviting different individuals to respond. Be familiar with the Scripture Notes at the end of this session.

2. How does anonymous hard work contribute to the unity within a body of believers—whether a church or small group—who follow Christ? How can befriending people contribute in powerful ways to any group?

3. Does the fact that we know little about Mary or Persis lower the value of their mention in Scripture? How would you feel if the Apostle Paul had mentioned you in this small way in his letter?

Some of those Paul greeted in his letters were unnamed but were still given prominence for their importance to his life and to Christ's work.

Greet Rufus, chosen in the Lord, and his mother, who has been a mother to me, too.

ROMANS 16:13, NIV

Some scholars believe that Rufus may have been the son of the Simon of Cyrene, the man who carried Jesus' cross. Simon is referred to as the "father of Alexander and Rufus" in Mark 15:21. That's certainly possible given Paul's reference that Rufus was "chosen in the Lord."

4. Of all the things Paul could have highlighted about Rufus' godly mother, why do you suppose he highlighted that she had been a mother to him? What important role can maternal figures play in the church?

Some women are known for having motherly hearts. Tender, concerned love flows from them in such a way that others are naturally drawn to their support. Remember, Paul spent his adult life traveling through the ancient world to spread the gospel of Jesus. He was persecuted, rejected, imprisoned, and attacked. A permanent home was not his to enjoy. Yet Paul knew the comfort of mother-love. In one unnamed woman, Paul found a substitute mother on whom he could rely.

5. Rufus' mother was referenced by the important role she played in Paul's life. Brainstorm a list of things for which mothers are known or credited. What does this list suggest about the influence of Rufus' mom in Paul's life?

6. There's an old adage: "There's no end to what you can accomplish if you don't care who gets the credit." Do you agree or disagree? Do you think most of us live as though we believe this saying? Explain.

Principle for Living
The value of your life is not measured by what you accumulate, nor by your fame or notoriety. "The LORD does not look at the things man looks at. Man looks at the outward appearance, but the LORD looks at the heart" (1 Samuel 16:7, NIV). Measure your life by the people you influence for good.

LIVING WITH THE IMPERFECT

There's truth in the saying, "If you find a perfect church, don't join it or it won't be perfect anymore." No study about the women in Paul's life could be complete without a look at Euodia and Syntyche, two ladies remembered not so much for their winsome testimonies as for the drama between them. In his letter to the Philippians, Paul writes:

So then, in this way, my dearly loved brothers, my joy and crown, stand firm in the Lord, dear friends. ² I urge Euodia and I urge Syntyche to agree in the Lord. ³ Yes, I also ask you, true partner, to help these women who have contended for the gospel at my side, along with Clement and the rest of my co-workers whose names are in the book of life.

PHILIPPIANS 4:1-3, HCSB

As you read verses 1-3, what sense do you get about Paul's personal relationship with Euodia and Syntyche? What's the tone of Paul's correction?

Paul referred to Euodia and Syntyche as women who "have contended for the gospel at my side." The Greek verb used for "contended" appears only twice in the whole Bible: here and in Philippians 1:27. It paints a picture of people involved in disciplined, diligent teamwork in spreading the gospel. Euodia and Syntyche were soldiers in God's army. Clearly, these two women were not contentious troublemakers; even faithful Christ-followers will have occasional clashes and disagreements.

Let the peace of Christ rule in your hearts, since as members of one body you were called to peace. And be thankful. ¹⁶ Let the word of Christ dwell in you richly … as you sing psalms, hymns and spiritual songs with gratitude in your hearts to God. And whatever you do, whether in word or deed, do it all in the name of the Lord Jesus, giving thanks to God the Father through him.

COLOSSIANS 3:15-17, NIV

Paul urged Euodia and Syntyche "to agree in the Lord." Considering Colossians 3:15-17 and your own life experience, what do you think Paul wants to see happen?

The disunity created by some disagreement or conflict was having a negative effect on the Philippian church. Paul called on these two godly women to "agree in the Lord." He did not mean that they needed to declare a winner in their dispute, but that they needed to allow the loving spirit of Jesus to guide their thoughts and words. Paul's goal was to redirect people to think about the larger story of being saved and adopted into the same family with our common bond in Jesus Christ rather than getting caught up in our smaller stories—our differences and our disagreements.

9. What are some "smaller stories" that we can get caught up in at church? At work? At home? How can focusing on these "smaller stories" affect our unity within the church and the effectiveness of our message to the people around us?

Principle for Living

We're all flawed. We all struggle, and we all fail. God is keenly aware of your humanness, but He delights in you and your messiness. In times of failure or difficulty, lift your eyes from your smaller story and fix your eyes on the larger story—the story of new life, of freedom, of healing, and of unity in Christ.

EMBRACING THE TRUTH

15-20 Minutes

LEADER: This section focuses on helping group members integrate what they've learned from the lives of these godly, but very real women into their own hearts and lives. Invite volunteers to read the Bible passages.

HOW TO BE A WOMAN OF HIGH ESTEEM

The women mentioned in Paul's letters had two things in common: they loved their Lord Jesus and they used what they had to join Him is His mission to a lost and hurting world. When you invite Jesus into your life, you become a new creation. It's time to put off the old you, the old habits, the old sins, and the old thought patterns that keep you trapped and ineffective. Instead, you develop a new attitude towards life and others that clearly reflects the love of Christ. Your life is no longer about you. Your deepest joy, your deepest fulfillment, your deepest significance comes from drawing closer to Jesus and letting Him live in and through you. As a faithful Christ-follower, you too are a woman whom Paul would hold in high regard.

Let's look at four key principles for becoming a woman of high esteem.

KEY 1: Recognize that your life prior to Christ is well lost; look to find your deepest joy and satisfaction in Him.

⁷ Whatever was to my profit I now consider it a loss for the sake of Christ. ⁸ What is more, I consider everything a loss compared to the surpassing greatness of knowing Christ Jesus my Lord, for whose sake I have lost all things. I consider them rubbish, that I may gain Christ.

PHILIPPIANS 3:7-8, NIV

1. The Apostle Paul penned his letter shortly before being killed for his allegiance to Jesus. What does Paul prize in the end? Why do you think this level of passion often eludes us?

2. In what ways can you demonstrate contentment and pleasure in your relationship with Christ? Why is it important that you do?

KEY 2: Happily live your life in service to Christ. Whatever your path, give it your all and enjoy the journey.

⁹ So let's not allow ourselves to get fatigued doing good. At the right time we will harvest a good crop if we don't give up, or quit. ¹⁰ Right now, therefore, every time we get the chance, let us work for the benefit of all, starting with the people closest to us in the community of faith.

GALATIANS 6:9-10, THE MESSAGE

3. Which of the following causes you to become weary in doing good?
   ○ Too much work or overwhelmed
   ○ An unbalanced lifestyle
   ○ Discouragement from others
   ○ An inability to discern God's direction
   ○ Doing tasks that are not suited to your gifts
   ○ Other: _____

   Explain.

4. What kind of harvest do you hope to see from your acts of service? What do you need to believe about God in order to continue doing good works even when you can't see any sign of a harvest?

KEY 3: Recognize that your identity and personal worth are tied to your relationship with Jesus. Don't worry about your looks or abilities; let your dedication to Jesus define how others view you.

²⁹ Many women are capable, but you surpass them all! ³⁰ Charm is deceptive and beauty is fleeting, but a woman who fears the LORD will be praised. ³¹ Give her the reward of her labor, and let her works praise her at the city gates.

PROVERBS 31:29-31, HCSB

Principle for Living
You will only find your identity, joy, satisfaction, and passion in Christ. While being commended by others is wonderful, we must always remember that our deepest heart's desire for acceptance and affirmation can only come from God.

KEY 4: You need to develop a deeper relationship and experience with God and increase in understanding His truth. But women of high esteem also point others to hope and healing in Jesus.

[15] Always be prepared to give an answer to everyone who asks you to give the reason for the hope that you have. [16] But do this with gentleness and respect, keeping a clear conscience.

1 PETER 3:15-16, NIV

5. Describe a time when you tried to share with someone about your faith. What steps can we take to become more effective at "accurately handling the word of truth" and being "prepared to give an answer to everyone" about the hope we embrace?

Just as these early church women modeled, we must be prepared and alert for "divine appointments" and "teachable moments" that will open the door to sharing with others about the hope and freedom in Christ. And when we do speak with others about Jesus, we must be sure to be patient and gentle ambassadors, careful to treat every person with the same kind of respect Jesus demonstrated.

Principle for Living

Every day you will meet people who desperately need to know God and discover the love, hope, freedom, and healing that comes from a new life in Christ. You have the incredible opportunity to show others the way of life! Be ready.

CONNECTING - *10-15 Minutes*

LEADER: Use connecting as a time to encourage and support one another as you each allow God room to work in your life.

IMPORTANT NOTE: Before you close this session of Held in High Esteem, *take a few minutes to discover what your group will do next to continue the journey toward redemptive community. When will you meet? What will you study or discuss? How will you stay regularly connected?*

LEADER INSTRUCTION FOR THE GROUP EXPERIENCE: Have a CD of worship music playing in the background. Ask the women to place their chairs in a large circle and invite one of the ladies to sit in a chair placed in the middle of the circle. Have each woman, one by one, take her place in that center chair. Ask the group to pray aloud for the woman in the center chair, as indicated.

As your leader directs, pray specifically for each woman in the prayer chair for these three things:

- Thanks for the woman's unique gifts and influence in the group
- Prayers for her spiritual growth and passion in her journey with the Lord
- A blessing over her current and future role in Jesus' mission

ADDITIONAL PRAYER REQUESTS:

TAKING IT HOME

LEADER: "Taking It Home" focuses on pointing others to the light of Jesus. Because this is the last meeting for this study, the temptation will be to skip this week's assignment. Encourage group members not to skip the questions to their hearts and to God this week. These may be the most important questions yet!

QUESTIONS TO TAKE TO MY HEART

The following question asks you to look into your heart and focus on your deepest feelings about yourself. Our behaviors are the best indicators of what we really believe deep down. Look deep into the underlying beliefs down in your heart where your truest attitudes and motivations live.

READ THE ARTICLE "I Stand at the Door" that begins on the next page, and then ask these questions of your heart.

❧ *How willing am I really to "stand at the door" for people? What is it that's driving my hesitancy, indifference, or even possibly my eagerness?*

❧ *What barriers in my life, and especially my beliefs, keep me from sharing with others about Jesus and the new life I've found in Him?*

I Stand by the Door [2]

By Sam Shoemaker, who helped draft the 12 Steps of A.A.

I stand by the door.
I neither go too far in, nor stay too far out,
The door is the most important door in the world-
It is the door through which people walk when they find God.
There's no use my going way inside, and staying there,
When so many are still outside and they, as much as I,
Crave to know where the door is.
And all that so many ever find
Is only the wall where a door ought to be.
They creep along the wall like blind people,
With outstretched, groping hands.
Feeling for a door, knowing there must be a door,
Yet they never find it ...
So I stand by the door.

The most tremendous thing in the world
Is for people to find that door—the door to God.
The most important thing any person can do
Is to take hold of one of those blind, groping hands,
And put it on the latch—the latch that only clicks
And opens to the person's own touch.
People die outside that door, as starving beggars die
On cold nights in cruel cities in the dead of winter—
Die for want of what is within their grasp.
They live, on the other side of it—live because they have not found it.
Nothing else matters compared to helping them find it,
And open it, and walk in, and find Him ...
So I stand by the door.
Go in, great saints, go all the way in—

Go way down into the cavernous cellars,
And way up into the spacious attics—
It is a vast roomy house, this house where God is.
Go into the deepest of hidden casements,
Of withdrawal, of silence, of sainthood.
Some must inhabit those inner rooms.
And know the depths and heights of God,
And call outside to the rest of us how wonderful it is.
Sometimes I take a deeper look in,
Sometimes venture in a little farther;
But my place seems closer to the opening ...
So I stand by the door.

There is another reason why I stand there.
Some people get part way in and become afraid
Lest God and the zeal of His house devour them
For God is so very great, and asks all of us.
And these people feel a cosmic claustrophobia,
And want to get out. "Let me out!" they cry,
And the people way inside only terrify, them more.
Somebody must be by the door to tell them that they are spoiled
For the old life, they have seen too much:
Once taste God, and nothing but God will do any more.
Somebody must be watching for the frightened
Who seek to sneak out just where they came in,
To tell them how much better it is inside.
The people too far in do not see how near these are
To leaving—preoccupied with the wonder of it all.
Somebody must watch for those who have entered the door,
But would like to run away. So for them, too,
I stand by the door.

I admire the people who go way in.
But I wish they would not forget how it was
Before they got in. Then they would be able to help
The people who have not, yet even found the door,
Or the people who want to run away again from God,
You can go in too deeply, and stay in too long,
And forget the people outside the door.
As for me, I shall take my old accustomed place,
Near enough to God to hear Him, and know He is there,
But not so far from people as not to hear them,
And remember they are there, too.
Where? Outside the door—
Thousands of them, millions of them.
But—more important for me—
One of them, two of them, ten of them,
Whose hands I am intended to put on the latch.
So I shall stand by the door and wait
For those who seek it.
I had rather be a door-keeper ..."
So I stand by the door.

Sam Shoemaker, founder of Faith At Work at Calvary Episcopal Church in New York City, in 1926, was also one of the spiritual leaders who helped draft the 12 Steps of A.A.

QUESTIONS TO TAKE TO GOD

When you ask God a question, expect His Spirit to guide your heart to discover His truth. Be careful not to rush or manufacture an answer. Don't write down what you think the "right answer" is. Don't turn the Bible into a spiritual reference book or encyclopedia. Just pose a question to God and wait on Him. Remember, the litmus test for anything we hear from God is alignment with the Bible as our ultimate truth source. Keep a journal of the insights you gain from your time with God.

    ❧ *God, what is about me that You esteem and appreciate?*

SCRIPTURE NOTES

OMANS 16:13

:13 Rufus. Quite possibly the son of imon of Cyrene, who carried Jesus' oss. Simon is identified (Mark 15:21) s the father of Alexander and Rufus.

HILIPPIANS 3:7-8; 4:1-3

7 profit ... loss. Paul describes his hange in outlook in terms of a balance heet. What was once on the "profit" de of the ledger (when he was a harisee) has been shifted over to the oss" side (now that he is a Christian).

8 compared to the surpassing greatness. aul discovered only one thing had any ltimate value—knowing Christ Jesus. nowing Christ did not come as a esult of any personal accomplishment.

2 urge. This is a strong verb, meaning o exhort, to implore, to beg." *Euodia ... yntyche.* Apparently these two women ad carried their quarrel into the ody, and it was threatening to split he church. Peace between them was rucial to the unity of the whole body.

the Lord. The only hope for this kind f unity to develop between these two omen is found in the fact and power f their common commitment to Jesus.

COLOSSIANS 3:15-17

3:15 Let the peace of Christ rule in your hearts. "Your" is plural: What is in view is not a sense of personal serenity, but a mutual commitment to consider peaceful relationships with one another as the highest priority in corporate life.

called to peace. While the reconciliation of people with God and one another is the major theme of Christian doctrine (vv. 9-11; 1:20-22; 2:2), living out this reconciliation is the major emphasis of Christian ethics (vv. 12-14; Rom. 14:19–15:7; Gal 5:22-26).

be thankful. Thankfulness for God's grace should be the central motive of Christian living (vv. 16-17; 1:12; 4:2).

3:16 the word of Christ. While the false teachers don't "hold on to the head" (2:19), the message that the Colossians teach must be centered on Jesus.

dwell in you richly. Spiritual fullness is rooted neither in secret knowledge nor in mystical experiences, but in a commitment to Christ.

admonish ... one another. The Christian faith is lived in community, not held in as a solely personal faith. All the aspects of worship listed here are to be carried out to build one another up, as well as directing our hearts toward God.

3:17 name of the Lord Jesus. Christ, the source of one's life with God (1:20,22), the One who is present with His people (1:27), the One through whom God is known (2:9), the One who rules over all creation (v. 1; 2:15), is also the model that people are to imitate in all areas of life. Thus Paul undermines the false teachers' assertions that Christ alone is inadequate for a full spiritual life.

PROVERBS 31:29-31

31:28-29 capable. This woman enjoys a good reputation not only in the community but also in her own household where her weaknesses are most evident.

31:30 praised. Beauty and charm are only temporary, but a life lived for the Lord is well remembered and worthy of praise.

31:31 city gates. A place where only men received recognition. This woman proves that good character and wisdom surpass gender and cultural bias.

SESSION QUOTATIONS:

1 "John Dobson" by Don Moser *Smithsonian*, November 2005, pp. 58-60. Excerpted from *Dynamic Preaching*.

2 "I Stand By the Door" accessed from www.faithatwork.com on 3/30/06 (Faith@Work™).
Used by permission.

Session Six

LEADER'S GUIDE

	PAGE
equired Session Supplies & Preparation	89-93
eading a Small Group	93-95
Velcome to Community!	96-100
roup Covenant	101
bout the Authors & Acknowledgments	102
Ieeting Planner	103
roup Directory	104

DISCOVER PURPOSE THROUGH THE JOURNEY
WITH OTHER COMPELLING STUDIES IN THE
WOMEN OF PURPOSE SERIES!

REQUIRED SUPPLIES AND PREPARATION FOR EACH SESSION

SESSION 1:

Supplies: - 2 large pieces of butcher paper
  - butcher paper cut in shapes of two life-sized women
  - colored markers

Procedure:
Before the group meeting, trace a life-size figure of a woman on each of two large pieces of butcher paper. Label one "Hypocrite Hannah" and the other "Sincere Sharise." Tape the cutouts up at the front of the room.

Question 3: As a group, brainstorm 10 things parents can do to contribute to a child's becoming hypocritical or spiritually apathetic. Write these on the Hypocrite Hannah cutout using the markers provided.

Question 4: Then, as a group, brainstorm ten ways parents can raise children to be sincere in their faith. Write these suggestions on the Sincere Sharise cutout.

SESSION 2:

Supplies: - one 6" x 6" square of red cloth for each participant
  - a fabric pen for each participant
  - colored markers

Procedure:
Ask group members to draw a heart on one side of the cloth. Then have them list inside the heart all the blessings they have received from giving their lives to Jesus. The backside of the cloth should be used as a place to write the names of those with whom they desire to share the life and hope found in Jesus Christ. Separate the women into small groups and ask them to share what they wrote on their pieces of cloth before praying together for one another.

Preparation

SESSION 3:

The Successful Woman ...

Supplies: - a stack of magazines related to pop culture and women's issues
- enough construction paper, scissors, and glue sticks for each pair of group members

Procedure:
Ask women to pair off with another group member. Look together through a couple of the magazines provided. Cut out titles and sentences that seem to embody our culture's philosophy of a "Successful Woman." Paste these to a piece of construction paper and then present them to the group.

A Walk to Remember ...

Supplies: - Have a TV/DVD player set up
- *A Walk to Remember* DVD (2002 starring Shane West and Mandy Moore)

Procedure:
Read the "A Walk to Remember" introductory paragraph and then show the end of Scene 26 "Father and son" through the beginning of Scene 28 "Her miracle" (1:29:28 to 1:35:02 on the DVD timer). Discuss the questions after viewing the scene.

SESSION 4:

Supplies: - Have a TV/DVD player set up
- *Spider-Man 2* DVD (2004 starring Tobey Maguire and Kirsten Dunst)

Procedure:
First, read the introductory paragraph to set up the FIRST clip. Then show Scene 48 "Web Love" (1:52:59 to 1:55:18 on the DVD timer). Discuss question 1 after viewing the first clip.

It's time to show the SECOND clip from *Spider-Man 2*. Show Scenes 50 "Here Comes the Bride" and 51 "The Final Swing," which ends the movie (1:57:99 to 2:02:30 on the DVD timer). Discuss the remaining questions.

Preparation

SESSION 5:

Supplies: - Have a TV/DVD player set up
 - *The Family Man* DVD (2001 starring Nicholas Cage)

Procedure: Read the movie introduction paragraph to set up the scene and then show Scene 15 (1:38:34 to 1:40:00 on the DVD timer). Discuss the questions that follow.

SESSION 6:

Household Gadgets ...

Supplies: - a variety of small household objects such as key chains, potholders, tape, flashlights, scissors, silverware, crystal creamers, spices, and candle

Procedure:
Ask participants to dig into their purses to contribute similar items to the collection you gathered before the meeting.

Ask each group member to choose from the collection of household items one thing that she feels best represents her spiritual journey. Invite each person to explain why she chose a particular item. It's okay if a couple of group members want to choose the same item.

Circle of Strength ...

Supplies: - a CD player
 - a worship music CD

Procedure:
Have a CD of worship music playing in the background. Ask the women to place their chairs in a large circle and invite one of the ladies to sit in a chair placed in the middle of the circle. Have each woman, one by one, take her place in that center chair. Ask the group to pray aloud for the woman in the center chair, as indicated. Instruct group members to pray specifically for each woman in the prayer chair for these three things:

• Thanks for the woman's unique gifts and influence in the group

• Prayers for her spiritual growth and passion in her journey with the Lord

• A blessing over her current and future role in Jesus' mission

Leading a Small Group

You will find a great deal of helpful information in this section that will be crucial for success as you lead your group.

Reading through this and utilizing the suggested principles and practices will greatly enhance the group experience. You need to accept the limitations of leadership. You cannot transform a life. You must lead your group to the Bible, the Holy Spirit, and the power of Christian community. By doing so your group will have all the tools necessary to draw closer to God and each other, and to experiencing heart transformation.

Make the following things available at each session:
- *Held in High Esteem* book for each attendee
- Bible for each attendee
- Snacks and refreshments
- Pens or pencils for each attendee

THE SETTING AND GENERAL TIPS:

1. Prepare for each meeting by reviewing the material, praying for each group member, asking the Holy Spirit to join you, and making Jesus the centerpiece of every experience.

2. Create the right environment by making sure chairs are arranged so each person can see the eyes of every other attendee. Set the room temperature at 69 degrees. If meeting in a home, make sure pets are in a location where they cannot interrupt the meeting. Request that cell phones are turned off unless someone is expecting an emergency call. Have music playing as people arrive (volume low enough for people to converse) and, if possible, burn a sweet-smelling candle.

3. Try to have soft drinks and coffee available for early arrivals.

4. Have someone with the spiritual gift of hospitality ready to make any new attendees feel welcome.

5. Be sure there is adequate lighting so that everyone can read without straining.

6. Connect with group members away from group time. The amount of participation you have during your group meetings is directly related to the amount of time you connect with your group members away from the meeting time.

7. There are four types of questions used in each session: Observation (What is the passage telling us?), Interpretation (What does the passage mean?), Self-revelation (How am I doing in light of the truth unveiled?), and Application (Now that I know what I know, what will I do to integrate this truth into my life?). You won't be able to use all the questions in each study, but be sure to use some from each.

8. Don't get impatient about the depth of relationship group members are experiencing. Building real Christian Community takes time.

9. Be sure pens and/or pencils are available for attendees at each meeting.

10. Never ask someone to pray aloud without first getting their permission.

LEADING MEETINGS:

1. Before the icebreakers, do not say, "Now we're going to do an icebreaker." The meeting should feel like a conversation from beginning to end, not a classroom experience.

2. Be certain every member responds to the icebreaker questions. The goal is for every person to hear his or her own voice early in the meeting. People will then feel comfortable to converse later on. If members can't think of a response, let them know you'll come back to them after the others have spoken.

3. Remember, a great group leader talks less than 10% of the time. If you ask a question and no one answers, just wait. If you create an environment where you fill the gaps of silence, the group will quickly learn they needn't join you in the conversation.

4. Don't be hesitant to call people by name as you ask them to respond to questions or to give their opinions. Be sensitive, but engage everyone in the conversation.

5. Don't ask people to read aloud unless you have gotten their permission prior to the meeting. Feel free to ask for volunteers to read.

6. Watch your time. If discussion time is extending past the time limits suggested, offer to the option of pressing on into other discussions or continuing the current session into your next meeting. REMEMBER: People and their needs are always more important than completing all the questions.

THE GROUP:

Each small group has it's own persona. Every group is made up of a unique set of personalities, backgrounds, and life experiences. This diversity creates a dynamic distinctive to that specific group of people. Embracing the unique character of your group and the individuals in that group is vital to group members experiencing all you're hoping for.

Treat each person as special, responsible, and valuable members of this Christian community. By doing so you'll bring out the best in each of them, thus creating a living, breathing, life-changing group dynamic.

YOU CAN HELP GROUP MEMBERS THROUGH ...

Support – Provide plenty of time for support among the group members. Encourage members to connect with each other between meetings when necessary.

Shared Feelings – Reassure the members that their feelings are very normal in a situation such as they are in. Encourage the members to share their feelings with one another.

Advice Giving – Avoid giving advice. Encourage cross-talk (members talking to each other), but limit advice giving. "Should" and "ought" to statements tend to increase the guilt the loss has already created.

Silence – Silence is not a problem. Even though it may seem awkward, silence is just a sign that people are not ready to talk. It DOES NOT mean they aren't thinking or feeling. If the silence needs to be broken, be sure you break it with the desire to move forward.

Prayer – Prayer is vital to personal and community growth. Starting and ending with prayer is important. However, people may need prayer in the middle of the session. Here's a way to know when the time is right to pray. If a member is sharing and you sense a need to pray, then begin to look for a place to add it.

Leading a Small Group

WELCOME TO COMMUNITY!

Meeting together with a group of people to study God's Word and experience life together is an exciting adventure. A small group is … *a group of people unwilling to settle for anything less than redemptive community.*

CORE VALUES

Community: God is relational, so He created us to live in relationship with Him and each other. Authentic community involves *sharing life together* and *connecting* on many levels with the people in our group.

Group Process: Developing authentic community requires a step-by-step process. It's a journey of sharing our stories with each other and learning together.

Stages of Development: Every healthy group goes through *various* stages as it matures over a period of months or years. We begin with the *birth* of a new group, deepen our relationships in the *growth* and *development* stages, and ultimately *multiply* to form other new groups.

Interactive Bible Study: God provided the Bible as an instruction manual of life. We need to deepen our understanding of God's Word. People learn and remember more as they wrestle with truth and learn from others. The process of Bible discovery and group interaction will enhance our growth.

Experiential Growth: The goal of studying the Bible together is not merely a quest for knowledge; this should result in real life change. Beyond solely reading, studying, and dissecting the Bible, being a disciple of Christ involves reunifying knowledge with experience. We do this by bringing our questions to God, opening a dialogue with our hearts (instead of killing our desires), and utilizing other ways to listen to God speak to us (group interaction, nature, art, movies, circumstances, etc.). Experiential growth is always grounded in the Bible as God's primary means of revelation and our ultimate truth-source.

Power of God: Our processes and strategies will be ineffective unless we invite and embrace the presence and power of God. In order to experience community and growth, Jesus needs to be the centerpiece of our group experiences and the Holy Spirit must be at work.

Redemptive Community: Healing best happens within the context of community and in relationship. A key aspect of our spiritual development is seeing ourselves through the eyes of others, sharing our stories, and ultimately being set free from the secrets and the lies we embrace that enslave our souls.

Mission: God has invited us into a larger story with a great mission. It is a mission that involves setting captives free and healing the broken-hearted (Isaiah 61:1-2). However, we can only join in this mission to the degree that we've let Jesus bind up our wounds and set us free. As a group experiences true redemptive community, other people will be attracted to that group, and through that group to Jesus. We should be alert to inviting others while we maintain (and continue to fill) an "empty chair" in our meetings to remind us of others who need to encounter God and authentic Christian community.

Stages of Group Life

Each healthy small group will move through various stages as it matures. There is no prescribed time frame for moving through these stages because each group is unique.

Birth Stage: This is the time in which group members form relationships and begin to develop community.

Multiply Stage: The group begins the multiplication process. Members pray about their involvement in establishing new groups. The new groups begin the cycle again with the Birth Stage.

BIRTH

MULTIPLY

GROWTH

DEVELOP

Growth Stage: Here the group members begin to care for one another as they learn what it means to apply what they have discovered through Bible study, shared experiences, worship, and prayer.

Develop Stage: The Bible study and shared experiences deepen while the group members develop their gifts and skills. The group explores ways to invite neighbors, friends, and coworkers to meetings.

Subgrouping: If you have more than 12 people at a meeting, Serendipity House recommends dividing into smaller subgroups after the "Breaking the Ice" segment. Ask one person to be the leader of each subgroup, following the "Leader" directions for the session. The Group Leader should bring the subgroups back together for the closing. Subgrouping is also very useful when more openness and intimacy is required. The "Connecting" segment in each session is a great time to divide into smaller groups of four to six people.

SHARING YOUR STORIES

The sessions of *Held in High Esteem* are designed to help you share a little of your personal lives with the other people in your group as you learn to parent well. Through your time together, each member of the group is encouraged to move from low risk, less personal sharing to higher risk communication. Real community will not develop apart from increasing intimacy of the group over time.

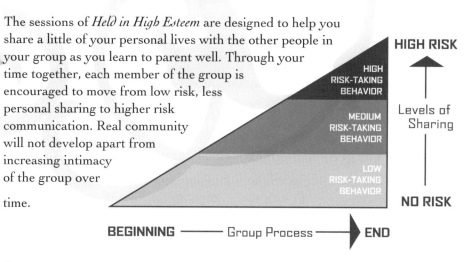

SHARING YOUR LIVES

As you share your lives together during this time, it is important to recognize that it is God who has brought each person to this group, gifting the individuals to play a vital role in the group (1 Corinthians 12:1). Each of you was uniquely designed to contribute in your own unique way to building into the lives of the other people in your group. As you get to know one another better, consider the following four areas that will be unique for each person. These areas will help you get a "grip" on how you can better support others and how they can support you.

G – Spiritual Gifts: God has given you unique spiritual gifts (1 Corinthians 12; Romans 12:3-8; Ephesians 4:1-16; etc.).

R – Resources: You have resources that perhaps only you can share, including skill, abilities, possessions, money, and time (Acts 2:44-47; Ecclesiastes 4:9-12, etc.).

I – Individual Experiences: You have past experiences, both good and bad, that God can use to strengthen others (2 Corinthians 1:3-7; Romans 8:28, etc.).

P – Passions: There are things that excite and motivate you. God has given you those desires and passions to use for His purposes (Psalm 37:4,23; Proverbs 3:5-6,13-18; etc.).

To better understand how a group should function and develop in these four areas, consider going through the Serendipity study entitled *Great Beginnings*.

Welcome to Community

99

GROUP MEETING STRUCTURE

Each of your group meetings will include a four-part agenda.

1. Breaking the Ice: This section includes fun, uplifting questions to warm up the group and help group members get to know one another better as they begin the journey of becoming a connected community. These questions prepare the group for meaningful discussion throughout the session.

2. Discovering the Truth: The heart of each session is the interactive Bible study time. The goal is for the group to discover biblical truths through open, discovery questions that lead to further investigation. The emphasis in this section is on understanding what the Bible says through interaction within your group.

To help the group experience a greater sense of community, it is important for everybody to participate in the "Discovering the Truth" and "Embracing the Truth" discussions. Even though people in a group have differing levels of biblical knowledge, it is vital that group members encourage each other to share what they are observing, thinking, and feeling about the Bible passages. Scripture notes are provided at the end of each session to provide additional Bible understanding.

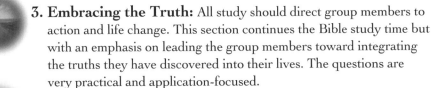

3. Embracing the Truth: All study should direct group members to action and life change. This section continues the Bible study time but with an emphasis on leading the group members toward integrating the truths they have discovered into their lives. The questions are very practical and application-focused.

4. Connecting: One of the key goals of this study is to lead group members to grow closer to one another as the group develops a sense of community. This section focuses on further application, as well as opportunities for encouraging, supporting, and praying for one another. There are also opportunities to connect with God and to connect with your own heart.

BONUS – Taking it Home: Between each session, there is some homework for group members. This typically includes a question to take to God and a question to take to your heart. These experiences are designed to reinforce the content of the session and help group members deepen their spiritual life and walk with Jesus.

Group Covenant

As you begin this study, it is important that your group covenant together, agreeing to live out important group values. Once these values are agreed upon, your group will be on its way to experiencing true Christian community. It's very important that your group discuss these values—preferably as you begin this study. The first session would be most appropriate.

Priority: While we are in this group, we will give the group meetings priority.

Participation: Everyone is encouraged to participate and no one dominates.

Respect: Everyone is given the right to his or her own opinions, and all questions are encouraged and respected.

Confidentiality: Anything that is said in our meetings is never repeated outside the meeting without permission.

Life Change: We will regularly assess our progress toward applying the "steps" to an amazing marriage. We will complete the "Taking it Home" activities to reinforce what we are learning and better integrate those lessons into our lives.

Care and Support: Permission is given to call upon each other at any time, especially in times of crisis. The group will provide care for every member.

Accountability: We agree to let the members of our group hold us accountable to commitments we make in whatever loving ways we decide upon. Unsolicited advice giving is not permitted.

Empty Chair: Our group will work together to fill the empty chair with an unchurched person or couple.

Mission: We agree as a group to reach out and invite others to join us and to work toward multiplication of our group to form new groups.

Ministry: We will encourage one another to volunteer to serve in a ministry and to support missions work by giving financially and/or personally serving.

I agree to all of the above_____ date: _____

About the Authors

More than 30,000 people currently attend Fellowship churches that Gene and Elaine Getz have planted in the Dallas area, while more churches span the globe. Dr. Gene Getz is a pastor, seminary professor, host of the "Renewal" radio program, and author of more than 50 books, including *The Walk*, *The Measure of a Man*, and *Building Up One Another*. Gene and Elaine recently released a revision of their best-selling book *The Measure of a Woman*. Elaine is a wonderful wife, mother, and grandmother, with much to pass on to younger women. The couple resides in Plano, Texas.

Acknowledgments

We truly appreciate the effective partnership between my team at the Center for Church Renewal and the team at Serendipity House, as well as all of the individuals who contributed to this effort.

We are deeply indebted to Iva Morelli and Sue Mitchell for their invaluable assistance in so many details of this and other projects.

My good friends at Serendipity House Publishing have again done a wonderful job in every aspect of this Women of Purpose study. We especially want to thank …
- Publisher Ron Keck for his vision
- Contributing writers Angela Akers and Ben Colter for working to develop this content into a small-group experience
- Brian Marschall for art direction and cover design
- The team at Powell Creative for design and layout of the interior
- Bethany McShurley and Ben Colter for editorial expertise
- Stacey Owens for an eye for detail

Regal Books, friends and partners in ministry, have graciously granted permission to include some content from *The Measure of a Woman* in this Women of Purpose series.

MEETING PLANNER

The leader or facilitator of our group is _____ .
The apprentice facilitator for this group is _____ .

We will meet on the following dates and times:

	Date	Day	Time
Session 1	_____	_____	_____
Session 2	_____	_____	_____
Session 3	_____	_____	_____
Session 4	_____	_____	_____
Session 5	_____	_____	_____
Session 6	_____	_____	_____

We will meet at:

Session 1	_____
Session 2	_____
Session 3	_____
Session 4	_____
Session 5	_____
Session 6	_____

Childcare will be arranged by: Refreshments by:

Session 1	_____	_____
Session 2	_____	_____
Session 3	_____	_____
Session 4	_____	_____
Session 5	_____	_____
Session 6	_____	_____

Meeting Planner

GROUP DIRECTORY

Write your name on this page. Pass your books around and ask your group members to fill in their names and contact information in each other's books.

Your Name: _____

Group Directory

Name: _____
Address: _____
City: _____
Zip Code: _____
Home Phone: _____
Mobile Phone: _____
E-mail: _____

Name: _____
Address: _____
City: _____
Zip Code: _____
Home Phone: _____
Mobile Phone: _____
E-mail: _____

Name: _____
Address: _____
City: _____
Zip Code: _____
Home Phone: _____
Mobile Phone: _____
E-mail: _____

Name: _____
Address: _____
City: _____
Zip Code: _____
Home Phone: _____
Mobile Phone: _____
E-mail: _____

Name: _____
Address: _____
City: _____
Zip Code: _____
Home Phone: _____
Mobile Phone: _____
E-mail: _____

Name: _____
Address: _____
City: _____
Zip Code: _____
Home Phone: _____
Mobile Phone: _____
E-mail: _____

Name: _____
Address: _____
City: _____
Zip Code: _____
Home Phone: _____
Mobile Phone: _____
E-mail: _____

Name: _____
Address: _____
City: _____
Zip Code: _____
Home Phone: _____
Mobile Phone: _____
E-mail: _____

Name: _____
Address: _____
City: _____
Zip Code: _____
Home Phone: _____
Mobile Phone: _____
E-mail: _____

Name: _____
Address: _____
City: _____
Zip Code: _____
Home Phone: _____
Mobile Phone: _____
E-mail: _____

Name: _____
Address: _____
City: _____
Zip Code: _____
Home Phone: _____
Mobile Phone: _____
E-mail: _____

Name: _____
Address: _____
City: _____
Zip Code: _____
Home Phone: _____
Mobile Phone: _____
E-mail: _____